The Dawning of
a Brighter Day

The Dawning of a Brighter Day

THE CHURCH IN BLACK AFRICA

Alexander B. Morrison

Deseret Book Company
Salt Lake City, Utah

This book is not an official publication of The Church of Jesus Christ of Latter-day Saints. No one asked me to write it. The views and ideas presented herein are my own and do not necessarily represent the position or view of the Church. Similarly, I also am fully responsible for errors and omissions in the text. All royalties received from sales of the book have been assigned to the Church Education System for African scholarship activities. — Alexander B. Morrison

Library of Congress Cataloging-in-Publication Data

Morrison, Alexander B.
    The dawning of a brighter day : the church in Black Africa / by Alexander B. Morrison.
      p. cm.
    ISBN 0-87579-338-X
    1. Church of Jesus Christ of Latter-day Saints — Missions — Africa, Sub-Saharan. 2. Mormon Church — Missions — Africa, Sub-Saharan. 3. Africa, Sub-Saharan — History — 1960- I. Title.
BV3520.M67 1990
266'.9367 — dc20   90-35883
                                            CIP

Printed in the United States of America

10   9   8   7   6   5   4   3   2   1

Contents

Acknowledgments

This book is dedicated to my beloved eternal companion, Shirley, whose faith in me is both humbling and inspiring. Our eight children (David, Barbara, Howard, Sandra, Allen, Jeffrey, Heather, and Mary) were convinced that "Dad could do it." I appreciate deeply their confidence.

It is difficult to list the names of all who provided assistance to me in writing this book. The many African members of the Church who have made me welcome and shared their testimonies; beloved missionaries whose examples of courage and faith have sustained me—all have my deepest gratitude and respect. So too do professional colleagues from many lands with whom I was privileged to associate in Africa over the years on World Health Organization committees. Val MacMurray, who shares a love for Africa, encouraged me to write the book. Elder Robert E. Sackley and his wife, Marjorie, provided invaluable insights and perspective gained from service as missionaries in Nigeria and freely shared both their knowledge and their love with me. Special thanks go to Elders Marvin J. Ashton, Neal A. Maxwell, and Jack H. Goaslind for their gentle, loving encouragement and sublime example. Carolyn Keight and Janet Morley typed the manuscript with skill and patience.

Africa, 1990

CHAPTER ONE

The Giant Behind the Veil

No part of the world has been so little understood as Africa. Most people in the United States, Canada, and other Western countries know that vast continent only through the distorted — or at least myopic — lens of television: hollow-eyed nomads fleeing their ancient enemies of drought and famine; vast fleets of zebra or wildebeest adrift on the grassy seas of the East African savanna; the exuberance of native dancers caught in a blur of motion and color. The reality of modern Africa is but little known to them. Few could name more than a handful of the several dozen countries found in Africa, and fewer still are aware of the complex constellation of historical, political, economic, and technological issues shaping Africa's future. Africa remains largely unknown to the West, a sleeping giant veiled in mystery and indifference.

Perhaps this is not too surprising. Until recently much of Black Africa was visited only by a handful of white traders and missionaries, whose stories about the "dark continent" largely were dismissed as romantic nonsense, tall tales too fantastic to be true. Furthermore, Africa is so huge and diverse that to know it well is extremely difficult. Its immense landmass is unexcelled in geographic diversity — ranging from trackless arid desert to dense tropical rain forest — and in the vast profusion of its plant and animal life. Occupying 20 percent of the

1

earth's land surface, it is four times larger than the United States and has twice as many people, divided into 2,000 tribes and ethnic groups, with hundreds of mutually unintelligible languages or dialects. It spans several time zones from east to west.

Communication across the continent, whether by air or telephone, is difficult at best. It is, for example, easier to fly from Monrovia, Liberia, to Nairobi, Kenya, by way of London than to go directly from one Africa city to the other, and telephone operators in Abidjan, Ivory Coast, simply refuse to book calls to Accra, Ghana, only a few hundred miles away. Road transport is both difficult and dangerous in most countries.

The name of the continent may come from the Latin word *Aprica* ("sunny") or the Greek word *Aphrike* ("without cold"), and its blazing heat in midsummer can sear the brain and blister the skin. Yet the cold of the Ethiopian highlands can leave one shivering and aching, with numb fingers and toes.

Africa is a continent of violent contrasts, with few constants and many contradictions, simultaneously repelling and enticing, presenting a myriad of discomforts and sorrows, both natural and man-made, along with great natural beauty. The peoples of Africa reflect the contradictions of the land itself. Stoic and long-suffering, they can be volatile and unpredictable. They are at once peaceful and truculent, wise and ignorant, friendly and suspicious, compassionate and indifferent.

The rusted bones of a burned-out bus lying by the side of the road between Accra and Cape Coast, Ghana, tell something of the volatility of the African villager, of how quickly his tranquillity can be drowned in a blood lust that sweeps all before it. A couple of years ago the bus, empty save for its driver and the ticket collector, ploughed into a procession of people marching along the road from one village to another to celebrate the birthday of a local chief. Several dozen people were killed or injured. The bus driver fled for his life, finally escaping from the irate survivors, but his unfortunate ticket collector, who went back to collect the fare box from the wrecked vehicle, was decapitated and thrown into the bus, which was then set on fire. Rough justice indeed!

Yet with it all, Africa has an ability to take hold of human hearts and minds. "It lays its hands upon you, and having once felt its compelling touch, you can never forget it," wrote an English admirer in the early years of this century. (Quoted in Basil Davidson, *The Story of Africa,* London: Mitchell Beazley International Ltd., 1984, p. 11.)

This is a book about one of the most spectacular events in the history of The Church of Jesus Christ of Latter-day Saints: the beginning of missionary work in Black Africa during the decade between 1978 and 1988.

In some ways, at least, I believe that establishing the gospel in Africa represents the most difficult challenge the Church has ever had to face. It goes without saying that our Father in heaven longs for our success there, as elsewhere. But even He has difficulty in inspiring us if we fail to do our homework. We will succeed in Africa only as we learn and come to understand the oftentimes confusing social, political, historical, and economic realities of that vast continent and base what we do on real knowledge. I am firmly convinced of the application to the work in Africa of the Lord's admonition to learn "of things both in heaven and in the earth, and under the earth; things which have been, things which are, things which must shortly come to pass; things which are at home, things which are abroad; the wars and the perplexities of the nations, and the judgments which are on the land; and a knowledge also of countries and of kingdoms — that [we] may be prepared in all things." (D&C 88:79–80.)

In the end, of course, after "all that we can do," we will succeed in Africa and elsewhere only to the extent we call upon the powers of heaven. This work cannot be accomplished without the Lord's help.

Before the story of the Church in Africa can be told, we

3

must deal with—and, it is hoped, dispose of—some commonly held myths and misconceptions about Africa, and learn about some of the real problems its people face.

Ancient African Origins

After centuries of dismissing Africa as "the dark continent," devoid of history or technology, its people backward, ignorant, and savage children of field and forest, Western society has at long last begun to appreciate something of the rich diversity and complexity of African history. This newfound understanding of the nature of Africa and its peoples reflects an older view. The ancient Greeks, for example, considered the black peoples of Africa to be different from them, but equal and at times even superior. Much of their knowledge of Africa related to Egypt, the "gift of the Nile," and its majestic civilization founded on the water and silt provided by the great river.

Current evidence suggests that Egypt was populated by black-skinned wanderers who came to the Nile Valley out of the Sahara, fleeing the drought that changed its green pastures and sweet rivers into a desiccated, barren wasteland roughly five thousand years ago. By the time of Sennacherib, king of Assyria (eighth century B.C.), Egypt was ruled by fierce warriors from the south, from the land of Kush. (See 2 Kings 19:9.) The capital city, Meroe, was founded near the current Sudanese capital of Khartoum, where the Blue Nile embraces its sister, the White Nile. The Kushites were farmers and herdsmen, men of the flock and field, who lived along the Nile and in the surrounding grasslands. Their civilization integrated local culture with that of the Egyptians; because they traded along the Red Sea and across the Indian Ocean, it included other more distant influences as well. Kush developed an important iron-smelting industry, and hence had iron tools and weapons, unlike the Egyptians, who used bronze. The Kushites also were one of the earliest peoples to develop an alphabetic script for writing purposes. Those who think that African history is in large measure devoid of technological advancements should be reminded that the Kushite script was as effective as that developed independently by the Greeks.

Kush remained a powerful factor in the development of Africa for three centuries after Christ. Philip the evangelist (Acts 8:26–29) met a high official of the Queen of Kush "on the way that goeth down from Jerusalem unto Gaza," explained the meaning of Isaiah 53:7–8 to him, "preached unto him Jesus," and baptized him. We do not know whether this trusted official took the gospel of Christ to his people, but Christian missionaries began to preach the gospel in modern Sudan in the fifth and sixth centuries A.D.

By about A.D. 350 Christian missionaries came to another part of eastern Africa, to the kingdom of Axum, which we know today as Ethiopia. Parenthetically, it is important to note that the biblical use of the term *Ethiopia* does not imply the modern country of Ethiopia. Biblical references to Ethiopia for the most part apparently relate to modern northern Sudan, the land of Kush. (See Isaiah 18:1.) By the fourth century the rulers of Axum began issuing coins of gold, bearing a Christian cross. Thus Christianity has been the official religion of Ethiopia for at least fourteen hundred years. When James Bruce of Scotland returned to Britain from his epic exploration of Ethiopia in the 1770s, he told of a kingdom with pomp and power, one whose king commanded an army of 30,000 men and who lived in lavish, luxurious splendor. Bruce was a proud and prickly man, and almost nobody believed him. After all, old boy, Africans couldn't be as advanced as Europeans, could they? We now know his accounts were generally accurate, and that Bruce was not only a very brave man, but an explorer possessed of unusual integrity and insight.

Black kingdoms flourished elsewhere in Africa, as well. Portuguese sailors, including Vasco da Gama and others who followed him around the southern tip of Africa and northward along the East African coast, soon heard of a great empire in

Scene in Ethiopia has changed little since ancient times

central Africa that was previously unknown to medieval Europe. This kingdom centered around the king's palace, or *zimbabwe*. In the Shona language, *zimbabwe* means royal court. At least two hundred palaces or courts were scattered around the countryside of present-day Zimbabwe and Mozambique. The largest was known as Great Zimbabwe. Its ruins reveal a massive enclosure with thirty-foot-high walls built of stones without cement. Many structures, also made of stone, were found within the walls, and a large number of mud and thatch huts were apparently located outside them, clinging like bedraggled children to their mother's skirts. It is generally agreed that Great Zimbabwe was built around A.D. 1200 by local Africans who possessed great skills as stonemasons. The wealth of the kingdom came primarily from long-distance trade of gold and ivory across the Indian Ocean, in return for cottons from India, silks and pottery from China, and glass from Arabia.

When Great Zimbabwe was excavated at intermittent intervals during the first half of the twentieth century, people were incredulous at the conclusions of the experts as to its origin. The idea that it might have been built by Africans boggled the minds of those who believed that Africans, intrinsically inferior children of nature, were incapable of major constructive effort. Surely, they said, Great Zimbabwe must have been built by the Arabs, or the Phoenicians, or the Queen of Sheba. Not so. All of the evidence indicates it was Africans who built the great stone city.

Far away from Great Zimbabwe, on the west coast of Africa, a series of splendid kingdoms developed, largely unknown to their contemporaries in medieval Europe. One of the greatest of these was the kingdom of Benin, described for a European audience by a Dutchman, Dierick Ruiters, who went there as a merchant shortly before A.D. 1600. He reported that the city of Benin in the kingdom of Benin (in which, incidentally, we now have several branches of the Church) was "very big," with a "big broad street, not paved, which seems to be seven or eight times broader than the Warmoes Street in Amsterdam. This street goes along straight without a bend; and where I was lodged . . . it was at least a quarter of an hour's distance from the gate, and yet I could still not see to the other end of the street. . . . The houses in this town stand in good order, one close and even with the other, as the houses stand in Holland. Those belonging to men of quality (which are gentlemen) have two or three steps to go up, and in front of each there is a kind of gallery where a man may sit dry. The palace of the king is very large, having within it many square courtyards with galleries around them, where sentries always stand." (Davidson, *The Story of Africa,* p. 77.)

Ruiters apparently concluded that the Africa city compared favorably with major European cities of the time.

Benin reached the height of its power in the fifteenth century, a hundred years or so before European traders and merchants began to visit that part of West Africa. At its zenith, the kingdom of Benin controlled a band of present-day Nigeria about 125 miles inland from the southern coast, and about 250 miles westward from the Niger River. The king, or *oba* (the office is still found in modern Nigeria), was believed to have divine sanction, though he was not considered divine himself, nor was he an absolute ruler. His authority came primarily from the prestige, awe, and mystery surrounding the office.

Europeans who visited Benin were favorably impressed by the civic order and general stability found there. A Dutch report from the early seventeenth century noted that the citizens of Benin "are people who have good laws and a well-organized police; who live on good terms with the Dutch and other foreigners who come to trade among them, and who show them a thousand marks of friendship." (Davidson, *The Story of Africa,* p. 82.) Portuguese traders and missionaries arrived in Benin before the Dutch, and Benin and Portugal even exchanged ambassadors in 1486.

Trade and Government

Another misconception about Africa is that until the last century or so, no commercial relationships existed between its kingdoms and those of Europe or elsewhere, and thus that Africa was isolated from the rest of the world in commercial terms. On the contrary, there is plenty of evidence that gold from Africa was being traded in Europe from very early historical times. The Phoenicians who founded Carthage in North Africa obtained gold from West Africa four centuries before Christ. Although the records of how this was accomplished are not extensive, it is apparent that trans-Saharan trade routes were used. By A.D. 1000, gold from West Africa provided the key to the economic success of powerful Muslim rulers who controlled a vast trading empire throughout the whole Mediterranean world and beyond. From Norman England throughout all of continental Europe, from Spain to India and even beyond to China, African gold fueled the fires of commerce. Gold, along with ivory and kola nuts (one of the few stimulants permitted by Islam), was exchanged for Indian cottons, Chinese musk (a substance obtained from the scent glands of the musk deer and used in making perfumes), swords of Damascus steel, English metalware, cloth, copper, and salt. A businessman in Cairo, for example, might use West African gold to buy copper or silk for sale in Timbuktu or another West African city.

The gold left West Africa from the great trading centers along the southern shores of the Sahara — Timbuktu, Gao, and Kano, among others — and arrived in Tunis, Tripoli, Alexandria, or Cairo after many weeks of portage by camel across the sea of sand. Stimulated by the gold trade, the economic activity in West Africa gave rise to a number of African kingdoms during the period from about A.D. 500 to A.D. 1500. A Moorish historian, al-Bakri, published in Cordoba in A.D. 1068 his *Book of the Roads and Kingdoms*, which drew upon travelers' and traders' reports to provide the following description of West Africa at that time:

"Ghana . . . is a title given to their kings; the region is Awkar, and their present king . . . rules an enormous kingdom, and has great power. . . . When he calls up his army he can put 200,000 men in the field, more than 40,000 of them archers. . . . When the king gives audience, or hears grievances against officials, he sits in a domed pavilion around which stand ten horses covered with gold-embroidered cloths. Behind the king stand ten pages holding shields and swords decorated with gold; and on his right are the sons of the vassal kings of his country, wearing splendid garments with gold plaited into their hair. At the door of the pavilion are dogs of an excellent breed. . . . Round their necks they wear collars of gold and silver." (Davidson, *The Story of Africa*, p. 90.)

The kings of Ghana taxed imports coming into or leaving their realm, operating a complex, sophisticated network of internal revenue collection. (Note: The kingdom of Ghana was not located in the country currently known by that name, but lay five hundred miles to the northwest, in the valleys of the upper Niger River.)

Over time one West African kingdom replaced another. In

the thirteenth century Ghana was succeeded by the empire of Mali, one of the largest states, being "four or more months' journey in length and as much in width." (Davidson, *The Story of Africa*, p. 91.) Mali had one of the richest systems of tax and tribute in the world outside of China and India. Soon after A.D. 1450, control over the trade routes passed to yet another group, the Songhay, who came from the region around the Niger River. Each of these succeeding dynasties was diverse in its composition, making room for all manner of local beliefs and loyalties and demanding little more for its rulers than tax, tribute, and ritualistic displays of submission.

Africa was the last of the continents to experience the full impact of European ideas and technology that dominated much of world history from the sixteenth to the early twentieth centuries. At the beginning of that period, Africa was far from being the most backward and primitive region on earth. Many African peoples were organized into states powerful enough to exploit their own resources, control their own trade, and deter invaders from Europe or elsewhere. It must, however, be admitted that before the later part of the eighteenth century most of Black Africa was little affected, at least directly, by the technological and scientific revolutions that transformed Western society. Whatever the causes — and there certainly were several, including accessibility, hostile climate, and the blight and burdens of disease in Africa — by the time of serious European exploration and colonization of Africa in the nineteenth century, Africa had fallen behind Europe and other Western countries in terms of technology.

Myths and Realities

From the foregoing it is apparent, however, that far from being ignorant primitives incapable of technological achievement or even of an ability to learn, Africans are as intelligent, capable, and talented as any other peoples around the world. We should not be surprised, therefore, by African investigators

Nigerian children, like children everywhere, enjoy blowing bubbles

who are eager to learn and quick to understand, nor by the ease and speed with which members of the Church in Africa learn Church procedures and operations.

Westerners tend to think of Africa as a continent of mud and thatch villages. Indeed, there are thousands of them. Village life revolves around its life-support systems — the drawing of water, the portage of food and firewood, cooking, washing, and petty trading. On market day hundreds of people converge on the square, like ants attracted to a sugar cube. Most are women, many bearing heavy burdens of firewood, bananas, and plantain or yams on their heads, but each walking with grace, beauty, and the dignity so characteristic of the women of Africa, young and old.

The overall impression of an African market is of a great jumble of noise, color, and confusion, overlaid with the rich and pungent odors of unwashed humanity, butchered goats and sheep, ripe fruits, and woodsmoke. There one finds people sleeping on or under tables cluttered with articles to sell; women with babies on their backs sewing cloth on hand-cranked sewing machines; food arranged in carefully con-

11

structed piles on the ground; the chatter of neighbors visiting and of vendors advertising their wares; the laughter of children at play—a small community with all of the color, gaiety, confusion, laughter, noise, and tears associated with everyday African life.

Most markets offer a wide variety of goods for sale, including locally made cloth in a profusion of colors and prints, yams, bananas, pineapples, garri (processed cassava), eggs and other foods, shirts and old shoes, secondhand automobile parts, tires, kerosene lanterns, a few canned goods—you name it and you can probably find it, at least on some days.

But Africa also is a continent of great cities. Over a dozen cities in Nigeria alone have a million or more inhabitants each, for example. In each, opulence and direst poverty live in close proximity, and Cambridge graduates rub shoulders with illiterate tribesmen. Each African city bulges at the seams, its numbers swollen by a constant migration of newcomers, predominantly young men. By the thousands each year they flee the farms and villages of rural Africa, looking for jobs in the cities. Too often, jobs are not available, and newcomers end up in squalid shanty towns hoping, where there is no hope, that tomorrow will be better. As a result of such chaotic growth, public services in African cities often are stretched beyond the breaking point, and street crime may be a major problem, although perhaps not much more so than in the inner cores of many American cities.

Most Africans are poor beyond the wildest nightmares of the vast majority of inhabitants of developed countries. Yet some have great wealth, the privileged few who control government and industry, who live in luxurious splendor and who send their children to North America or Europe to be educated. An educated and relatively affluent middle class of merchants and professionals is beginning to emerge in some African countries. Such is the flexibility, ingenuity, and mutual interdependence of Africans that even the poor manage to get by some-how, most of the time.

Yet Africa has the resources to be prosperous. It has 40 percent of the world's potential hydroelectric power supply and nearly 10 percent of its known petroleum reserves and natural gas. Sub-Saharan Africa is a mineral bonanza of unex-celled abundance and diversity, rich in copper, cobalt, dia-monds, manganese, chromium, and many other minerals. Geo-logically, Africa's potential for production of minerals is equal to, if not greater than, that of other continents. Nor do its people have to starve: properly utilized, Africa's millions of acres of untilled farmland could provide all of the food needed by her burgeoning population, and to spare. Corruption, mismanage-ment, ignorance, and indifference deny millions of Africans their right to basic necessities taken for granted in developed countries.

I believe that the needed catalyst for change is now at hand. The restored gospel of Christ, with its unparalleled power to lift and leaven, to sanctify and cause men and women to reach their full potential as human beings, can bring needed change to Africa. Indeed, I am convinced that only the gospel of Christ can save Africa. The schemes of men, no matter how well-intentioned, will not do so. Science and technology, despite their power to do good, will not suffice. Africa's salvation, like that of the rest of the world, lies not with the arm of flesh, but in the sweet fruits of the gospel.

Its benign, beneficent influence can already be seen in the lives of thousands of converts to The Church of Jesus Christ of Latter-day Saints in Black Africa. That influence will roll on, inexorably, undeterred, inevitable, until God's children in Af-rica can "come unto Christ, and be perfected in him." (Moroni 10:32.)

CHAPTER TWO

African Society: Tradition and Change

M any factors in African life in-
fluence the growth of the Church there. These include tribalism,
the undervaluing of women, the power of the extended family
unit, the hunger for education, the African zest for business.
and a natural spirituality and love of religion. It is not possible
in a work such as this to go into great detail concerning these
factors, but an overview should help give some perspective to
the challenges we face.

Tribalism

Tribalism is one of the most potent forces in African life.
It pervades every aspect of African society, is a major factor in
wars and power struggles, and at the day-to-day level deter-
mines who is hired or fired, who receives government largesse,
who goes to university, who "looks down" on whom. Publicly,
it is deplored by African politicians, but all of them, from top
to bottom, practice it.

To most Africans, loyalty to the extended family — making
sure that you and yours are looked after first — is far more
important than any nebulous loyalty to the nation. That primary
loyalty is expressed in a myriad of ways. Given the antipathy —
often hatred — between tribes located within national boundaries, it is no wonder, for example, that national leaders choose

14

their close advisers and trusted confidants from their own tribes, and make certain that those from other groups are deliberately kept away from the levers of power.

The contempt with which African tribesmen hold those who are "strangers and foreigners" is elegantly summed up in the creed of the Maasai herdsmen of Kenya and Tanzania. Their legends say they came from the north where, writes author Dino Sassi, "the earth is sand over which a great river flows, and no-one knows where this river ends. There was no grass for the cattle in that land, and no food for the people, so the Maasai had to look for another place, further south." (Dino Sassi, *Maasai,* Keasta, Nairobi, 1979, p. 4.) In the sixteenth century they found their home in the plateaus of the Rift Valley between Lake Victoria and Mount Kilimanjaro, which they revere as the home of the gods. There they warred against their farmer neighbors, despised creatures who owned no cattle, and thus, to Maasai eyes, beings beyond contempt. The Maasai enjoy the certain assurance that they are favored above all others. "God has entrusted the cattle of the earth to us because the Maasai are the best and the strongest people. Only the Maasai can live off cattle, which is the greatest form of wealth, and the others must content themselves with the fruits of the earth, because they do not know how to raise cattle like the Maasai. It is a sin to cultivate the earth and an offence to God." (Ibid., p. 7.)

Mistrust and suspicion between neighbors in Africa is not limited to competing black tribes. If anything, the antipathy across racial groups is even greater, as illustrated by the troubled relationships between blacks and Asians in East Africa.

The Asians in Africa live, and have lived for many years, in a sort of no-man's land. They first came to East Africa in the 1700s as traders, often the first contact the African villagers had with foreigners. Their relationship with their black neighbors has always been an uneasy one. Many Asians have thought the Africans to be lazy and ignorant, and the Africans in turn have considered the Asians manipulative and cunning. Asians were brought by the thousands to eastern and southern Africa as indentured servants, after slavery was abolished in the nineteenth century. They worked in the sugar plantations of South Africa, built the railway from Mombasa (Kenya) to Uganda and from Beira (Mozambique) to southern Rhodesia (now Zimbabwe), and labored as agricultural workers all over East Africa. Many arrived after the two world wars, seeking a better standard of living and a better future for themselves and their children than they would have had in Karachi or Bombay. They were segregated residentially and commercially by colonial governments, supposedly for "sanitary" reasons, but probably because to do so made it easier to keep them under close supervision and control.

But the Asians possessed several advantages that soon resulted in their controlling much of the economy of East Africa. They were industrious, shrewd, and aggressive traders and merchants, individuals who did not hesitate to exploit the ignorance of their black neighbors. They put considerable stress on educating their children. Of equal importance, they learned quickly to circumvent the barriers imposed by a white-dominated society and, in the process of mastering "the system," emerged as the money brokers and rich merchants of East Africa.

The blacks have resented the success of the Asians and have been angered by their unwillingness to force changes by embracing black nationalist movements. In 1972, Idi Amin of Uganda expelled all Asians from Uganda on ninety days' notice. Although the national economy soon collapsed, some Africans turned a blind eye to the human rights implications of what was happening and cheerfully applauded Amin's efforts.

Elsewhere in the 1970s other African governments acted in similar ways to drive out the Asians or curtail their economic power. In the past few years, pressure on the Asians has quietly lessened, as governments have belatedly realized that contin-

16

ued participation of the Asians in their economies is essential, but few Asians have any illusions of being loved by their black neighbors.

Tribalism involves far more than doing minor favors for your family and friends, or even of seeking protection for them. The essence of tribalism is power — the power to determine someone else's place in life, to offer employment, to provide favorable terms or conditions, to control another's future. Those who are powerless and who depend upon the favors of a dispenser of power become unable to exercise their own moral agency, unable to think for themselves, afraid to make decisions on their own. The average African man, caught in the terrible heritage of tribalism, is little used to making his own decisions and depends upon others to make them for him.

To some extent, the weak sense of nationhood and continued strength of tribalism in Africa is related to the colonial era of African history, when European diplomats and bureaucrats arbitrarily carved out nations by drawing lines on a map of Africa without reference to the ethnic homogeneity of the peoples involved. The callous disregard of the colonial powers for the wishes of the African people is well illustrated by events of October 1884, when delegates from fourteen countries (pointedly not including any Africans) met in Berlin at the Conference of Great Powers to decide the fate of Africa. Four months later, in February 1885, they signed the General Act of the Berlin Conference, which effectively partitioned Africa among the European governments concerned by establishing spheres of influence. Although this reduced direct rivalries between the European powers, the resultant mishmash of tribal groups, often containing those who were hereditary enemies, made nation building a difficult task indeed.

The national boundaries established were illogical and artificial, designed for the benefit or convenience of the Europeans and totally indifferent to the cultural heritage of centuries

17

Children in Nigeria learn at early age how to grate cassava, an important staple food

that had held African peoples of similar ethnic background together through the ties of language, common history, and shared culture. For example, the Maasai, those great warriors of the East African grasslands, were divided arbitrarily between British-ruled Kenya and German-ruled Tanganyika. The Shona tribe of southern Rhodesia had no natural affinity for their Ndebele neighbors, with whom they were forced to become reluctant partners in an artificial nation.

Under such circumstances it is no wonder that people continued to give their first loyalties to the tribe rather than the nation.

The dark and bloody side of tribalism is well illustrated by the periodic slaughter of Hutu peasants in Burundi, a tiny, land-locked, impoverished state located in East-Central Africa. Four centuries ago, the Hutu, small, thick-set chocolate brown farmers who make up 85 percent of the population of Burundi, were conquered by the tall, slim, haughty cattle herders of the Tutsi tribe. Since then the Tutsi have treated the Hutu majority

18

as serfs, ruling them with an iron hand and contemptuous disdain. An abortive Hutu uprising was drowned in a river of blood in 1972, when approximately 100,000 Hutus were massacred by their fellow countrymen. In 1988, a petty quarrel led to the killing of two Hutu, and in revenge the Hutus tried once more to rise against their Tutsi masters. The Burundi army, composed almost totally of Tutsi, slaughtered thousands of helpless Hutu, and at least 35,000 refugees fled to neighboring Rwanda in fear of their feudal overlords.

Given the pervasive influence of tribalism in Africa, it is not surprising that the Church's activities have been affected by it, both positively and negatively. Indeed, failure to come to grips with tribalism would doom our efforts, as it has those of so many others in the past. For example, one of our chapels in a West African country was defaced by vandals. The mission president turned the matter over to the state police, and one of their officers eventually received a confession from two individuals. Said he to the mission president, "I can't arrest these two, even though they have confessed, until I receive permission from the chief." The chief, in turn, indicated that he would personally question the men, who were members of his own tribe. Having done so, he reported to the police officer that the men were innocent! In reporting the matter to the mission president, the police officer simply said, "I can do nothing." Case closed.

It is not uncommon for a chief to say to our missionaries, "Come to my village. All of my people will join your church." Under such circumstances it can be taken for granted that the villagers are prepared to join the Church because of pressure from the chief, rather than because of individual conversion. Parenthetically, in Africa, as elsewhere, true conversions occur when individual souls, one by one, make personal decisions and then come to Christ with broken hearts and contrite spirits. Without putting too fine a point on it, an offer by a chief to have all of his village join the Church must always be viewed

19

with a certain amount of skepticism. It may be related to his desire to sell the Church land for a building, enhance his personal political prestige, or some other less-than-holy reason.

The other side of the coin also is not uncommonly encountered—a chief who doesn't want us in his village, who says, "My people will not attend your church. I have told them not to." Perhaps a chief who acts in this way does so out of a sense of pique, because we have refused to accept his offer of a "bargain" price on land, or have turned down some other proposal he considers too good for Church leaders to refuse. In one instance, a branch president had been chosen in the usual way and sustained unanimously by the congregation. The chief, who was not a member of the Church, objected, and within days the branch began to disintegrate, with those who had sustained the branch president refusing to do as he asked in righteousness, under pressure from the chief. The chief even wrote to the mission president demanding that the branch president be removed from office. In doing so, the chief was simply fulfilling his perceived role and right to control everything of any importance in his village.

In yet another episode, a local branch president, with great courage, publicly defied the chief and refused to go along with his attempts to subvert and undermine the local priesthood leadership. The branch president was attacked verbally and physically by the chief's supporters. The mission president wisely and courageously closed the branch, refusing to be bullied. After several weeks, the chief backed down, and the entire congregation came back to church!

The point is not that it is better to have the chief for us rather than against us. Whether the chief is pleasant or otherwise is not the issue. Problems are bound to arise if he perceives he has a right to interfere with the operations of the Church. Of course, not all the chiefs do so. Many are fully supportive of the purposes of the Church and, even if not convinced of the value of the Church on spiritual grounds, can see the practical benefits for their people often associated with membership in it.

Over the years our mission presidents in Africa have wisely and successfully challenged and defeated the power of tribalism. They do so primarily in two ways. First, they adamantly refuse to bow to unrighteous demands of local chiefs. They do not let others set our agendas or determine our priorities, and they maintain independence from others at all costs, including shutting down a local branch, if need be. This takes courage and resolution, but there can be no substitute for it. How blessed we are that our mission presidents possess the needed strength and determination.

The second key to dealing with tribalism is to build strength in the cities rather than in the villages where tribalism is most powerful and where there is little movement of people in or out, educational standards tend to be lower, and the traditions of centuries are maintained. In the large cities, the power of tribalism in inherently weaker. Those who have the courage to move to the cities and leave the security of the village have, to some extent at least, indicated a willingness to break with the traditions of the past. The melting-pot nature of the cities, which brings together people of various ethnic–tribal backgrounds, and in which people are required to think more for themselves in order to survive, is less conducive to maintaining the power of tribalism. As we concentrate our proselyting in the cities of Africa, we encounter much less tribalism, which one wise African leader, President Daniel arap Moi of Kenya has termed "the cancer that threatens to eat out the very fabric of our nation."

The Role of Women

The women of Africa are the great unsung heroines. Noble, undervalued, and unappreciated, they are the most important factor in food production, the mainstay of the economies of rural communities, the hewers of wood and the drawers of

Nigerian woman
and her child

water. Long hours of labor and few comforts are their daily lot. Yet the women are those above all who hold the family together, who nurture and sustain. They bear and raise the children, make most of the family decisions, grow, harvest, market, and cook most of the food, and in a myriad of ways serve as the hubs around which families revolve and as the cement that glues African society together.

To say that the African woman is undervalued is putting it mildly. She is unlikely to inherit anything if her husband dies, and indeed in such circumstances may well end up, along with her children, being displaced from the family home. She is considered not as a companion of her husband, but as a chattel. Her daughters are bought and sold in marriage, as she was.

Woman carries load
of wood on her head

She often is mistreated by her husband, who usually feels no compunction about beating her. She is in every sense a second-class citizen, whose primary responsibility is to produce babies and to work.

I think of two African women who typify the lot of their sisters across the continent. I met one of them a few years ago in Ivory Coast, near a village 250 miles up-country from Abidjan, the capital. I was there as a consultant with the World Health Organization, visiting an area where there had been a dangerous flare-up of African sleeping sickness. She was crossing the Bandama River, wading half-way up to her knees in the water, which was shallow because it was the dry season. She was five months pregnant, carried a baby on her back, cradled a toddler on one hip, and had two preschoolers tagging on behind. Her free hand grasped a rusty machete, and a battered basket of bananas was balanced on her head. She was hot, dusty, sweating, and tired — but smiling and happy as she shook hands with me.

23

Also in Ivory Coast, I recall a village woman — she could have been twenty or forty — pounding the hulls from rice with a wooden mortar and pestle almost as tall as she was. It was midday in June, hot and humid. She was covered with dust from the grain and her face was streaked with sweat, the muscles of her arms and shoulders glistening and rippling as she rhythmically put all of her strength into each stroke of the pestle. She looked so tired and hot that my heart went out to her. In the shade of the trees nearby sat the men of the village, smoking their pipes or ruminating over the state of the crops or the latest village gossip, none of them lifting a hand to help her. In Africa, as in many other places, it's a man's world!

As they investigate The Church of Jesus Christ of Latter-day Saints, the men of Africa are taught to treat their wives "even as Christ . . . loved the Church." (Ephesians 5:25.) Sometimes they need to be reminded of their duties, but they learn fast. One of our mission presidents noticed, just a few minutes before a district conference was to start, that all of the men were seated inside in the shade, while all of the women and children were outside in the broiling sun. "Brethren," he announced, "we won't start conference until you're seated with your families." It took only a few minutes for the changes to be made and for an important lesson to be learned, not to be forgotten.

A fine man joined the Church in Nigeria and shortly thereafter pledged to his wife, for the first time in his life, that he would be faithful and true to her, that he would no longer get drunk and mistreat her, and that he would stop wasting family funds by irresponsible spending. He was true to his word. Said she to me a few months later, "Now I have a real man!" Of course, not all African men behave badly toward women. How thrilling it is to see the great love many African men have for their wives. A classical love story is that of Ike and Patience Ikeme, recounted in Chapter Six.

The Extended Family

If there is one area in which we in the West can learn from Africa, it is in caring for each other within the family unit. The Africans excel at looking after family members. If one person works, a dozen eat. The concern spreads beyond parents and siblings, to include cousins, uncles, nieces, and nephews. The young, the old, the sick—all receive love and care, food and shelter, as long as there is a family member who can provide aid by sharing and giving.

I recall the night watchman (the "watchee-night") at our mission home in Lagos, Nigeria, a few years ago. He was a Hausa, from the north of Nigeria, a tribe well known for its martial prowess and warrior status. Armed with a machete and a whip, he patrolled the mission compound after dark, and I for one wouldn't have wanted to quarrel with him. Each night, about nine o'clock, he built a fire just outside the compound gate and cooked his simple evening meal. Soon, drifting like wraiths out of the darkness, coming from I know not where, there arrived a good half-dozen members of his extended family, young and old, male and female, to share a common meal and experience anew the powerful emotions of love and family solidarity.

African children are deeply loved. Strapped on their mothers' backs from their earliest days, they accompany them as they collect firewood, carry water, work in the fields, or travel to the market. The bond between mother and child is very close, and physical development of African children during the first year of life is precocious compared to that of American or British children. By the end of the second year, however, the mother usually has had another baby, and the first is left to fend for itself, with the aid of older siblings who pack the younger ones around on their backs, keep them away from the cooking fires, and help them to scrounge for tidbits and scraps as best they can. Small wonder that toddlers are most vulnerable to the malnutrition, parasites, and diarrhea that

25

Children carry water
in jars to their homes

plague African families and cause the deaths of so many millions of African children each year.

African children are very respectful of their elders and would never dare to question their authority. Perhaps that is one reason why African sacrament meetings are so quiet. Everyone, children and adults alike, watches the speaker with intense, rapt concentration. There is no squirming on the benches, no wandering in and out for drinks of water, no visits to the restroom. Under such circumstances the level of spirituality in sacrament meetings is high.

Perhaps another reason why Africans listen so intently in sacrament meetings is that theirs is an oral rather than an archival, or written, tradition. Many African societies have had written records only during the last century. The emphasis on remembering what has been said perhaps helps explain why our native African missionaries memorize scriptures much more readily than do most missionaries.

The weakness of the African archival tradition is linked to the weakness of its calendar tradition. Many Africans do not know how old they are or even in what year they were born. This causes significant problems for the Church's record-keeping system, requiring great efforts from branch clerks and others to maintain records in proper form and content.

Education

The great dream of African parents is that their children get an education, so they can at least read and write and do simple arithmetic. With education, they hope, will come better opportunities for jobs and enhanced security, perhaps even a job with the government, considered by many to be the ultimate prize. Tragically, unemployment levels are so high in most African countries that many of those with a good education still cannot find work. Yet they hunger to learn, undergo great sacrifices to stay in school, and haunt the few bookstores in the cities.

I think of an elementary school in a rural community a few miles from Harare, Zimbabwe, which I visited one rainy morning with Joseph Hamstead, our mission president in Zimbabwe, and his wife, Margaret. We left the road and bumped along a farm track, the wheels of the car slipping and sliding in the mud from the overnight rains. The school building was an abandoned beer hall, made of mud-brown homemade concrete blocks and fitted with a rusted roof of corrugated iron. There were no windows, so the doors at each end of the building had to be kept open to allow some light in. Of course, the rain came in as well, running in brown rivulets across the dusty floor. There were about twenty-five children in each of two classrooms, separated by a partition of used flour sacks sewn together and strung from a wire stretching across the room. The children were of mixed ages—between six and twelve, I would guess. All of them were barefoot, the boys in short trousers and faded T-shirts, the girls in worn dresses. All were thin and ragged looking. Many had walked three to five miles to school that morning, across the farmland and along the forest paths, probably without breakfast. There were no desks. To write, each child knelt on the wet, cracked concrete floor and used the seating bench for a desk. Each pupil had the stub of a pencil and one sheet of paper, but no textbooks or readers. They watched us with grave solemnity but smiled when we asked them to sing for us. Many were Latter-day Saints, and it was thrilling to listen to them sing "I Am a Child of God." Then they sang, with touching sincerity, the "national hymn" of Africa—"Lord, Bless Africa."[1] I thought to myself, *Yes, God bless Africa, and God bless you too, my dear little ones whom He loves so much. You are His children. You are the hope of the future. You will help shape and guide your great country. You have so little and need so much. God bless you.*

An outstanding characteristic of the growth of the Church in Black Africa is that it is attracting large numbers of educated potential leaders. It is as though the Lord has led us to those of His elect who will serve as the seedstock for future growth of the Church in Africa. To illustrate, in mid-1988, of the district presidents in Ghana and Nigeria and the members of the presidency of the newly formed Aba Nigeria Stake, all but two were university graduates. That is not to say, of course, that God places inordinate emphasis on worldly education. Indeed, as Paul noted: "God hath chosen the foolish things of the world to confound the wise; and God hath chosen the weak things of the world to confound the things which are mighty." (1 Corinthians 1:27.) Nevertheless, at this stage of our work in Africa, when development of priesthood and sister leadership is so important, it is significant that so many converts are already partially prepared to accept leadership responsibilities. It is, I believe, a great miracle. Unlike many educated people in Western countries, educated Africans do not turn from God, but rather seek to learn more of Him.

---

[1]The words of this great song tell much about Africa and Africans. The first verse, for example, reads in part as follows: "Lord, bless Africa, / Hear thou our prayers / And bless us."

Dealing and Trading

Africans are born traders and deal makers. They love to negotiate and haggle over prices and know to the last penny how much an item is worth. The dickering involved is all done in great good spirits. It is seen as a game to be played, a challenge of wills to be won, a respite from boredom. On a recent visit to Nigeria I recorded the dialogue in one such transaction. It went as follows:

"Oh Mastah, buy this from me. I give you good price."

"How much do you want?"

"Twenty-five nairas [about $3]."

"Too much. I will not pay."

"Oh Mastah, tell me *your* best price. I give *best* price, cheap, cheap."

"Ten nairas."

"Oh Mastah, that is too little. You are not serious. I give it to you for twenty-four."

"Sorry, forget it. Too much. I will buy from someone else."

"Oh Mastah, take it now, from my hand. Buy it from me. I give you fifty-year guarantee. Buy it from my hand."

"I will give you twelve nairas, top price — no more."

"Oh Mastah, I cannot do it. I must feed my family."

"Sorry. Good-bye."

"Mastah, come back; I give it to you for sixteen nairas. I like you."

"Make it fifteen."

"Bring money, Mastah."

In this transaction, have no fears that the seller was hoodwinked by the buyer. If anything, the reverse is true: African traders know to the farthing what they must sell at in order to make a profit and will not be coerced or persuaded into selling for less. They just do not make bad deals, at least from their point of view.

All of this trading and negotiating, which reveals the great potential of Africans to conduct successful businesses, given

Market scene
in African village

the opportunity, has its greatest importance for the Church in issues of principle. In a desperately poor society, principles may seem to some to be luxuries people cannot afford, but Church leaders must refuse to negotiate on issues of principle. Any evidence that they are unsure of their position, or any indication that their views can be changed, will generate persistent attempts to "strike a deal." If Africans sense they can negotiate—on tithing, the Word of Wisdom, marriage patterns, or a host of other issues—they, like most other people, will attempt to do so. Leaders thus have a great responsibility to teach correct principles and to set personal examples of unfaltering integrity.

Religion

Africans are by nature spiritual. Perhaps their innate spirituality is enhanced and reinforced by closeness to the eternal rhythms of nature with which most of them live their lives. Africans see God's handiwork around them every day, in the workings of nature, the stars in their places, the seasons, plant-

30

ing and harvesting. All remind them that "the heavens declare the glory of God; and the firmament sheweth his handywork." (Psalm 19:1.) It is difficult indeed to find an African who is an atheist. I for one have never known such a creature.

To Africans, the existence of God — in whatever form belief in Him may be expressed — is a self-evident truth. Religious discussions are thus as common as those about the weather or yesterday's football game.

Because Africans are not ashamed of or embarrassed by discussions about religion, it is perhaps not surprising that many decorate their trucks, taxis, or automobiles with religious slogans or use religious motifs in naming their businesses. Some examples noticed during a recent visit to Nigeria include the following:

"God of Mercy Truck" on a giant transport truck.

"Immeasurable Grace" on a taxi.

"God Is All" on the back bumper of an auto.

"Mother of God Maternity Hospital" over the front door of a building.

"Son of Man Motors" on the front window of an automobile dealer's establishment.

Three great religious traditions are found in Black Africa, existing together, often in the same community. The first is animism, a form of pantheism indigenous to Africa, which attributes a soul to natural objects, such as a tree, a river, a rock, or a mountain, all of which may be worshipped. Many millions of Africans, particularly those in villages and rural areas, still practice this ancient native religion.

Islam, the second great religious tradition in Africa, came to West Africa with caravans of Arab merchants during the eighth or ninth century A.D. It took root slowly, but during the eleventh century it became accepted by West African kings, who found it could accommodate a wide variety of local loyalties and customs. Other than requiring acknowledgment of a single God and the unique role of the prophet Mohammed,

Islam demanded relatively little of the people. Islam has continued to spread throughout Black Africa, particularly in West Africa. Today, for example, estimates of Nigeria's Islamic population range from 30 to 50 percent of the total. Indeed, of the three largest tribes in Nigeria, at least half of the Yoruba and almost all of the Hausa are Muslims. Similarly, black nations such as Mali, Niger, Sierra Leone, the Gambia, and Senegal are predominantly Muslim. Christian-Muslim antagonisms simmer close to the surface in many of these countries. As our membership base broadens and deepens in Black Africa, we will inevitably be required to expand our interaction with our Muslim brothers and sisters, reaching out to them in love, sensitivity, and mutual respect.

As already indicated, Christianity came to East Africa — to Ethiopia and the Sudan — some fifteen centuries ago. Elsewhere in Black Africa, Christian missionaries arrived on the heels of the first white explorers. Roman Catholic missionaries from Portugal and Spain came to Africa in the sixteenth and seventeenth centuries, but as the secular power of Portugal and Spain declined, so too did their ecclesiastical energies in Africa. French Catholic missionaries, notably the White Fathers and the Congregation of the Holy Ghost, and other missionaries from Germany and Britain brought various versions of Christianity to Africa in the nineteenth century. David Livingstone, the great Scottish explorer of Africa, was a missionary whose account of his travels, published under the title *Missionary Travels and Researches,* aroused the zeal of Victorian England for the opening up of West Africa to Christianity and commerce — not necessarily in that order, I might add. Today, thousands of Christian groups of all persuasions are in Africa. Many are in reality a mixture of traditional Christian beliefs with native African religions.

We owe a debt of gratitude to other Christians who came to Black Africa before members of The Church of Jesus Christ of Latter-day Saints did. They prepared the soil for us, helping to assure that the fullness of the gospel message that we bear would fall on receptive ears. We can and must learn from their experiences. It is significant that essentially all of our converts in Black Africa are coming to us from other Christian churches. They often know their Bible well. They love Christ, insofar as they know Him; and having received part of the truth, they are eager to embrace all of it. They quickly come to love the Book of Mormon and the other Restoration scriptures. They have but to hear the fullness of the gospel to believe it.

Throughout the history of the Church, it has been common for converts to feel they were led to it by divine influences. Many have had premonitions they would receive a great message at some time in the future — information of transcendental importance that would lead them to Christ and His salvation. That feeling of premonition, of anticipated blessings, is extremely common among African converts, many of whom have dreamed they would someday hear a glorious message that would change their lives forever. One of our earliest converts in Nigeria, Brother Anthony Obinna, for example, was not surprised when he first saw a picture of the Salt Lake Temple. He had seen it, he said, in a dream several years before.

The experience of Sister Mishika Dbinga, an African woman living in Ivory Coast, further underlines the great spirituality of the African people and their susceptibility to spiritual influences. Seeking a church that she could attend and to which she could give her heart, Mishika visited various Pentecostal churches in the area of Abidjan where she lives. Though others around her were exuberant and ecstatic in their religious fervor, she felt only an empty and dark feeling in those sectarian meetings. Her former husband had been a Muslim and so she attended Muslim services, still trying to find a faith in which she could believe. Though she appreciated the piety and sincere belief of many who attended those meetings, she could not share their fervor and, in fact, felt only an emptiness.

A friend introduced her to The Church of Jesus Christ of

Latter-day Saints, and as soon as she began to take the missionary lessons, the feelings of darkness and depression that had haunted her left at once. Fears she had had of staying alone in her house at night also went away, and she now sleeps soundly.

Sister Dbinga became committed to baptism, and just prior to the last missionary lesson, she had a vivid dream that profoundly affected her. In the dream the Savior appeared to her three times in a single night. On each occasion He said, speaking in French, "Mishika, will you come unto Me?" She answered, "*Oui*"—Yes.

She came to her baptism exhilarated and radiant with the memory of the dream uppermost in her mind. The African member who attempted to baptize her was relatively inexperienced and failed on three occasions to conduct the ordinance properly. Brother Scott Taggart, an expatriate missionary working in Abidjan, actually baptized Sister Dbinga. She was thrilled that he baptized her. She had prayed, she said, that Brother Taggart would be the one to carry out that sacred ordinance on her behalf, and she felt certain that God had intervened to answer her prayers. She is a fine and very devoted sister who has a deep testimony of the gospel of Christ.

To most Africans, the veil between this world and the next is extremely porous. The belief that spirits from the next world can be conjured up readily to enter this one, with good or bad results for the health and well-being of those affected, is taken for granted. It is the basis for the power of native healers and of charismatic native preachers, who invoke the spirits—both good and bad—of the dead at will, or so the people at least believe. Charismatic religious leaders, known and regarded as prophets, who are able to bring forth the spirits and converse with them and who regularly have so-called visions and visitations, garner immense followings, numbered in the millions. Such persons tend almost inevitably to invoke their own charismatic powers, rather than those of an institutional church, in

Young women
getting ready for church

dealing with their flock. Thus, mainline Christian churches have experienced great difficulties in maintaining discipline in some of their African leaders and members, whose religious orientation reverts readily to Africanism and away from Christianity.

The African belief that the departed can and do communicate with the living strikes a familiar chord with members of The Church of Jesus Christ of Latter-day Saints. Indeed, we believe that the salvation of the dead is necessary for our own salvation (see D&C 128:15), and communication with dead family members, while not an everyday occurrence, is not viewed as impossible or even improbable. Thus parents report that dead children have appeared to them with messages of reassurance about their well-being, and departed spouses may counsel the living wife or husband.

35

Speaking on this topic, President Joseph F. Smith said on one occasion: "We begin to realize more and more fully, as we become acquainted with the principles of the gospel, as they have been revealed anew in this dispensation, that we are closely related to our kindred, to our ancestors, to our friends and associates and co-laborers who have preceded us into the spirit world. We cannot forget them; we do not cease to love them; we always hold them in our hearts, in memory, and thus we are associated and united to them by ties that we cannot break, that we cannot dissolve or free ourselves from. . . . [They] can see us better than we can see them — . . . they know us better than we know them. . . . I claim that we live in their presence, they see us, they are solicitous for our welfare, they love us now more than ever." (*Gospel Doctrine,* Salt Lake City: Deseret Book, 1966, pp. 430–31.)

Africa, then, is a hotbed from which spring new religions of every belief and orientation. Into this pulsating blend of some truth mingled with error, superstition, and apostasy, The Church of Jesus Christ of Latter-day Saints has come to Black Africa. It brings the fullness of the glorious gospel of Jesus Christ, restored to the earth for the last time. Its message falls upon receptive ears. Praise be to God, there are millions of our Heavenly Father's children in Black Africa who are anxious to hear the truth.

Elder Robert E. Sackley, a member of the Second Quorum of the Seventy, has said: "I have noticed that the intellectual African is searching for God. By contrast, the intellectual North American often tends to become interested in something other than God. Nigerians read their Bibles continually. They are deep believers in the Lord. . . . I would say if Africa has any message for us, it is that education ought to bring us closer to God and not further away from Him. It has done so here [in Africa]. The educated blacks of Western Africa are inclined to reach for the spiritual things. They do not separate their intellectual studies from their spiritual lives. As they study, they become more deeply aware of the expanse of the universe and all that the Almighty God has created." (*Church News,* May 21, 1988, p. 7.)

Under the inspired direction of our prophet-leaders, the Church will continue to grow in Black Africa, and it will be in the Lord's way, not man's way. Despite all of its problems and traditions, Africa is now ready to hear and accept the gospel message in its purity and fullness.

CHAPTER THREE

In the Furnace
of Affliction

It has been said that Africa is shown as green on many maps because the verdant foliage has been watered by the tears of its people. Many millions of Africans are trapped in the furnace of affliction, the victims of problems that directly or indirectly influence the ability of the gospel message to take root in African soil. These problems include the following.

Health and Disease

In addition to the diseases of temperate climates, inhabitants of tropical African countries bear the added burdens of such tropical diseases as malaria, river-blindness, and schistosomiasis. Such diseases frequently lead to early death but invariably result in debilitation and intense chronic suffering. Though their victims most frequently are children, they affect people of every age. They can disable an entire population, cause the abandonment of fertile and productive land, and prevent the planting or harvesting of crops.

For example, the rainy season, when African farmers must work their land, coincides with the peak of malaria transmission. If a farmer is sick from malaria, he cannot work, and he and his family may starve. Since antimalarial medication costs too much for routine use, many sufferers are caught in a deadly cycle: they are sick because they are poor, and poor because they are sick.

In addition to their effects on health, tropical diseases have a marked inhibiting effect on social and economic development. Healthy people are required for development, and development is needed to provide the financial and other resources on which improved health is based.

Many tropical diseases play important roles in the cycle linking infection with malnutrition. They contribute to malnutrition, which in turn decreases resistance to the diseases themselves. Malnutrition saps energy and motivation and reduces performance in school and at work. In the developing countries of Africa, as many as 25 percent of the people have food intakes below the critical minimal levels. The burden of malnutrition, of course, falls most heavily on the poor.

Diarrheal diseases, transmitted by fecal contamination of water, food, and soil, are estimated to kill over two million African children each year. Perhaps the single action leading to greatest improvement in public health in Africa would be to provide a safe, regular water supply to inhabitants of all countries. At present, only about 65 percent of city dwellers in Africa have dependable access to reasonably safe, clean water and adequate sanitary facilities. In rural areas, fully 80 percent of the people lack ready access to clean, safe water.

In its humanitarian services work in Black Africa, The Church of Jesus Christ of Latter-day Saints has placed major emphasis on providing clean water for the people. In central Kenya, for example, a community water system, bringing clean water to some 10,000 people, has been completed recently at Ngorika, with extensive financial assistance from the Church. The project involved the laying of nearly fifteen miles of four-inch steel pipe, construction of water tanks, and providing hook-ups from the main lines to individual homes. Much of the work was done by the local inhabitants, who have formed a cooperative society to operate what is in effect a municipal utility company. The Church has also sponsored clean-water projects in Nigeria, where we have had extensive well-drilling operations, and in Ghana and Zimbabwe.

The heaviest burdens of disease in Africa fall on the children. Malaria is estimated to kill one million African children under the age of twelve each year. The common infectious diseases of childhood, which have, in the main, been reduced to relatively minor problems in developed countries, continue to exact heavy tolls in Africa. Mortality from measles, for example, may reach 20 to 30 percent in a malnourished population of African children, whereas measles only rarely causes serious problems in well-nourished American children. Despite herculean efforts by many governments, only about one-half of African children born each year are immunized against the common diseases of childhood.

The Church has contributed significantly to immunization programs for children in Africa. In Kenya, for example, in cooperation with Rotary International, one million doses of polio vaccine are being provided for use in the government's immunization program, and in Ivory Coast 600,000 doses of the vital vaccine have been donated for use by the government.

The specter of AIDS (Acquired Immune Deficiency Syndrome) broods over Africa and threatens the future. Current information on the epidemiology of the disease in Africa has been summarized by Dr. Jonathan Mann, former director of the Global AIDS Program of the World Health Organization (WHO), and his associates. (See "The International Epidemiology of AIDS," *Scientific American,* October 1988, pp. 82–89.) They report that the best and the brightest individuals — in short supply in any country, but especially so in the emerging nations of Black Africa — seem most at risk from AIDS. Although only some 15,000 AIDS cases were reported to WHO from Black Africa during 1987, the actual total was acknowledged to be much higher. The cumulative total of AIDS cases in Africa to mid-1988 was estimated at more than 100,000, and WHO estimated that more than a million Africans had been infected by the AIDS virus, and that 30 percent of these will develop the disease within a few years. The situation since 1988 has only gotten worse in Africa. Tragically, there is no real hope of a cure in the next decade, if ever.

In Africa, as elsewhere, AIDS is primarily a sexually transmitted disease. In addition, however, no Black African country can assure the quality of the national blood supply, and Africans who accept blood transfusions run a real risk of infection with AIDS virus.

In many of the cities of central African countries, including Uganda, Zaire, Zambia, and Tanzania, from 5 to 20 percent of the sexually active age group has already been infected by AIDS virus. Close to half of all patients hospitalized in such cities are infected with the virus, and 25 percent of hospital deaths are AIDS-related. Child mortality rates can be expected to increase by as much as 50 percent over the next few years, effectively wiping out hard-won gains made in child survival over the past twenty years. By the early 1990s, adult mortality rates in African cities will have doubled or trebled as a result of AIDS. At least 400,000 new cases can be expected in the next five years in urban centers of Africa, and if the disease spreads to rural areas, where 80 to 90 percent of the total population lives, that figure could skyrocket. Even 400,000 new cases will simply overwhelm the health care systems in developing African countries. A disaster of gigantic proportions is possible in the future.

Most African governments are extremely reluctant to talk about AIDS among their citizens. Their reluctance is a compound of fear, anger, and shame: They fear the loss of tourist dollars and of foreign aid, they are angry at what many Africans see as a conspiracy by Western countries to blame Africa for a worldwide plague, and in traditionally modest African societies they are ashamed to talk about the sexual connotations of AIDS. Indeed, in the Swahili language AIDS is said to stand for *aibu imeingia duninani sasa,* meaning "shame has fallen on the earth." It is, of course, impossible to predict what the long-term effects of AIDS will be in Black Africa, but there is reason to fear it will ravage a continent already heavily burdened with more than its share of problems.

Health problems in Black Africa are exacerbated by the fact that in most countries health workers are in extremely short supply. Burundi, for example, has approximately 45,000 people per physician, and Senegal over 15,000, as compared to approximately 500 people per physician in most Western countries. Other health care professionals are also in extremely short supply.

A few statistics illustrate the effects of all of this misery. The average life expectancy at birth is about seventy-two years in developed countries such as the United States or Western Europe, but in Africa it is only about fifty years. Of every 1,000 children born into poverty in Africa, 125 die within a year, another 100 die before the age of five, and only 500 survive to the age of forty. Infant mortality rates are ten to twenty times higher in Black African countries than in Western countries such as the United States. The World Health Organization has estimated that about one-tenth of the life of an average person in a developing country in Africa is seriously disrupted by disease.

The combined effects of disease, malnutrition, and poverty on the peoples of Black Africa are well illustrated in several small villages I visited a few years ago in Burkina Faso, a small, dry, and very poor country north of Ivory Coast and west of Niger. Unlike their neighbors in Niger, where much Arab influence is found, the inhabitants of Burkina culturally are much like those in the northern portions of Ivory Coast, although the major ethnic group, the Mosi, have more of an Arab cast to their features and fewer negroid characteristics than their forest-dwelling neighbors to the south. The land is typical African savanna — patchy grasslands with a few thorn bushes and the ubiquitous baobab trees, which, with their characteristic squat, thick trunks and sparse leaves, are well adapted to a region of little rainfall. The further north one goes in the country, the drier it becomes, as the searing heat of the Sahara presses ever closer.

At the time of my visit in June 1985, the farmers of Burkina were in serious trouble. The crops had largely failed the previous year, the granaries were empty, and the children were thin and listless. No harvest could be expected until December at the earliest. At one village, Wyen, there had been a rain shower three days previously, and the farmers, gambling that serious rains would follow, had sown their treasured and irreplaceable hoard of seed grain. If more rain didn't arrive in the next two or three weeks, the seeds would be lost and the farmers would be in terrible trouble. Yet with the fatalism of the African peasant, they had made a decision and would literally live or die by its consequences.

How I admired their courage. I thought, How quickly "civilized" Western man has become separated from the roots that bind him to the soil of mother earth. How quickly we forget our dependence on the beneficence of nature. How artificial our lives have become. These simple, illiterate peasants make life-and-death decisions each year without the sophisticated, computer-assisted technology we in the West think so necessary. Are we, after all, so clever, or have we lost something of importance as we move ever further away from the land and the sky and the rhythms of nature?

The villagers were very poor, dressed in rags, and everyone looked tired and apathetic. As usual the children were beautiful, with beautiful brown eyes and lovely smiles. I thought of how their beauty would soon shrivel and wither under the merciless pressure of poverty and illness, and my heart ached for them. A small boy had the enlarged liver and spleen of malaria, and there were, I was told, blind persons in the village, though not people who were both old and blind. Those who are both

Typical home in rural Africa

blind and old tend to die off quickly in a subsistence economy where all hands are needed constantly just to keep body and spirit together.

A very old and pathetically frail man tottered up on stick-like legs to peer at me. His leathery, lined face, thatched conical hat, and one-piece garment that looked like a butcher's smock made him appear like a figure out of another world. His legs were like pipe-stems, not more than two inches in diameter at the ankle, and I noticed he had the "tiger shanks" — areas of whitish depigmentation on his legs — characteristic of onchocerciasis (river blindness). He was not totally blind, though I had the definite impression his vision was impaired. Not that there was much worth looking at around the village. Indeed, the village itself was hard to see from a distance, the dried-mud huts blending into the drab monotony of the landscape. There was not a living plant, not a blade of grass or tree or shrub for at least a mile or more in any direction from the village.

Wyen is a village that ten years ago was full of river-blindness victims, many of them blind. Thanks to a major international effort to control the blackflies that spread river blindness, none of the children are now affected clinically, though at least some of the adults who were infected a decade ago still carry the parasitic worms that cause the disease.

To those who are shocked by the terrible infant mortality in Africa, who weep at the loss of millions of lovely children each year, it is, I believe, natural to ask heart-wrenching questions: What good does it do to help? If through herculean efforts we are successful in decreasing infant mortality in Black Africa through proper nutrition, diarrheal disease control, and immunization, have we simply postponed disaster? Will the children die anyway in a few years from starvation or infectious disease?

Before considering that specific question, it is important to consider a more generic issue. Why, as a church and as individuals, should we be concerned with temporal problems in developing nations such as those in Africa? After all, our resources, both temporal and otherwise, are already claimed at home, and even if we applied all that we have to Africa's problems, we, as a church and people, still couldn't meet all of its needs. Yet even asking the question outrages our hearts. What kind of people would we be if we failed to respond to suffering and want? Of course we must help. We cannot do otherwise if we are to lay claim to being our brother's keeper and disciples of the Master.

Aggregate needs may indeed be overwhelming, but hunger and pain are experienced individual by individual. In the same way, we can relieve some needs individual by individual. To help one person is better than helping no one. To refuse to help one person because we cannot help one hundred is, in some respects, self-indulgence, a refusal to acknowledge our own limitations and to grieve for them even as we attempt to reduce them. In this regard, I think of Mother Teresa, holding the hand of a dying man and giving him the only gift she had, the gift of dying "within the sight of a loving face." She did not have the medical resources necessary to reclaim his life nor the food to reverse the debilitating malnutrition that had sapped his strength before disease came; but she did not, for that reason, think that what she had was not enough. "We ourselves feel that what we are doing is just a drop in the ocean," she conceded, "but if that drop was not in the ocean I think the ocean would be less because of that missing drop." (Malcolm Muggeridge, *Something Beautiful for God: Mother Teresa of Calcutta*, Garden City, New York: Doubleday & Company, Inc./Image Books, 1977, pp. 31, 92.)

The fundamental reason why we must help in Africa lies in the charge Christ has given to us to love and care for each other—the divine injunction to "love one another, as I have loved you." (John 15:12.) We simply cannot claim to fulfill that commandment if we, as the apostle James gently points out, see "a brother or sister . . . naked, and destitute of daily food, and . . . say unto them, Depart in peace, be ye warmed and filled; notwithstanding ye give them not those things which are needful to the body. . . . Faith, if it hath not works, is dead, being alone." (James 2:15–17.)

Our responsibility as a church and people is great, not only to contribute to the Christian work of service, but also to make our own unique contribution. Elder Neal A. Maxwell pointed out that distinctive contribution at a gathering in 1976 to discuss our international expansion. Said he, "The Church constitutes a distinct alternative to the world. We are a counter-culture. . . . And our whole assumption is that we change the world by changing individuals. Ours is the original gospel of hope." At the same conference, Noel B. Reynolds, then chairman of BYU's Philosophy Department, went further and said, "As the gospel comes to men, it presents them with a radical alternative to the world views to which they have previously been exposed. . . . The gospel does have its own world view, teaching men that everything in this world was created by God, that men themselves are . . . spirit children of their Father in

Group of Latter-day Saints in African branch

heaven, and that obedience to his commandments as received through personal revelation takes priority over any require-ments of a traditional culture." ("Selected Remarks: Excerpts from 'The Expanding Church' Symposium," *Ensign,* December 1976, pp. 14–16.) As Latter-day Saints we must manifest that difference, not by excluding Christian charity from our legit-imate field of interests, but by making it a focus of our gospel teaching.

Now to return to the specific question: Are babies in Africa, if they don't die in infancy, doomed to die anyway within a few years from starvation or disease? There are many reasons why such need not occur, and all argue for a multidisciplinary approach to improving health. First of all, it is literally true that "the earth is full, and there is enough and to spare." (D&C 104:17.) The maximum capacity to produce food in Black Africa has by no means been reached. At household or community levels, production of nutritious foods necessary for health can be increased significantly if the people are shown what to do and given the proper incentives. Similarly, much can be done to teach families to adjust patterns of food intake and reduce food losses from pests and inadequate storage facilities. There

47

is, of course, a finite maximum capacity of Africa — or the entire world, for that matter — to produce food, but that is far from being reached at present.

Second, the impact of infectious disease can be reduced markedly. Appropriate use of currently available immunization technology would do much to reduce the incidence of infectious diseases of childhood, and clean water and improved sanitation would significantly reduce the overall burden of disease in both children and adults. Finally, in many poor areas, where large percentages of children die before reaching a productive age, uncertainty about who will care for parents in their old age and the overcompensation it induces have been found to be significant factors in determining family size. Thus, if fewer children die, family size can be expected to show moderate spontaneous decreases.

The health problems described above certainly apply to vast numbers of people in Black Africa, most of whom are poor and uneducated. But what about expatriate Westerners, such as missionaries who go to Africa for relatively short periods of time? Is their health also at risk?

Black Africa 150 years ago aptly was termed "the white man's graveyard." The average life expectancy of explorers, missionaries, military men, and traders who went to Africa from Britain and other European countries in the mid-nineteenth century was probably less than twelve months. In the main they died from malaria, yellow fever, and other insect-borne tropical infections. The mordant humor of an old scrap of English doggerel verse crystallized the fears of the whites: "Beware and take care of the Bight of Benin;[1] / For one that goes out there are forty go in."

Today, however, thanks to advances in medical and public health knowledge, Westerners, including our missionaries,

---

[1]The Bight of Benin includes that portion of the Atlantic Ocean stretching eastward from Takoradi in Ghana to the mouth of the Niger River in eastern Nigeria.

who go to Black Africa need not be concerned inordinately about their health. Precautions must still be taken. Yellow fever immunization is essential in most countries of West and Central Africa, and antimalaria tablets must be taken faithfully. Drinking water must be boiled or treated chemically, and care must be taken to ensure that all food is safely prepared, cooked, and refrigerated. Cleanliness in personal hygiene and sanitation is essential. But if these sensible, simple precautions are taken, our missionaries need not worry about their health. They will be as healthy in Africa as at home.

Nor need our missionaries feel for a moment that they will not get enough good quality food to eat. African fruits and vegetables are unexcelled in quality and variety. Local fish and meat, if properly cooked and refrigerated, are both safe and tasty. Bread and other cereal products are of high quality. A broad variety of canned food products from many countries is available — certainly not in the same profusion and assured supply as in Western supermarkets, but available nonetheless. Since supplies are variable, experienced shoppers soon learn to stock up on canned foods and other household products when they are available — a practice fully compatible, by the way, with the admonition of Church leaders to store a supply of food and other essentials for "a rainy day."

Literacy

In the absence of literacy, it is extremely difficult to preach the gospel, read the sacred scriptures, raise the standard of health, or help people to help themselves by improving their economic status, living standards, sanitary standards, and so on. An ability to read and write enables people to understand their temporal and spiritual problems and ways to solve them. Furthermore, it helps them to solve practical, everyday problems at the household and community level.

The adult literacy rate is, for practical purposes, nearly 100 percent in developed countries, but is only approximately 25 percent in African countries. Given the important role women play in education within the home, it is particularly tragic to note that only approximately 13 percent of women in Black Africa are literate. Only four out of every ten children in Africa complete more than three years of primary school.

Poverty

Perhaps the root cause of most of the problems just described is poverty. Although the gross domestic product (GDP) is by no means an ideal economic indicator, in general, citizens of countries with a high GDP have high life expectancy and low infant mortality rates. The reverse is true for countries with a low GDP. In developed countries such as the United States, the GDP is approximately twenty thousand dollars per person per year. In Black Africa, by contrast, the GDP hovers around the equivalent of three hundred to eight hundred dollars per year. A recent publication by the World Bank underlines the dire economic straits in which Africans find themselves. In 1987 the total gross domestic product of 450 million people in Black Africa was approximately equal to that of the 10 million who live in Belgium. (*Sub-Saharan Africa: From Crisis to Sustained Growth*, Washington, D.C.: World Bank, 1989, p. 2.) In many countries in Black Africa per capita income is actually expected to decrease over the next few years.

Population Growth

In the developing countries of Black Africa, nearly half of the people are under fifteen years of age, and thus largely economically unproductive, as compared to approximately 23 percent in the same age group in developed countries.

There is a continuing trend toward urbanization, as thousands of people each year leave rural areas and flood into cities. Lagos, the capital of Nigeria, for example, has grown from 300,000 to more than three million inhabitants in the last decade. Continuing urbanization in Africa has important socioeconomic and health effects. As people crowd into the cities, disease patterns change. Heavy additional burdens are placed on physical and social infrastructures, food production and distribution systems, housing, sanitation, water supplies, and health care.

Famine

As one of the Horsemen of the Apocalypse, famine has been our almost constant companion throughout history. One of the earliest recorded famines occurred in Africa. The Old Testament (Genesis 41) records that Joseph, falsely imprisoned in Pharaoh's dungeon, was able to interpret Pharaoh's dreams and predict that after seven years of plenty a terrible famine would sweep over Egypt. He proposed a grain storage program ("and Joseph gathered corn as the sand of the sea"), which protected the people of Egypt when the famine "waxed sore." It appears others were not as provident as Joseph, since it is recorded that "all countries came into Egypt to Joseph for to buy corn; because that the famine was so sore in all lands." (Genesis 41:57.)

The biblical story of famine in Egypt underlines some important facts about famines. They have occurred throughout all of recorded history. They are often associated with war. Although they are exacerbated by acute natural disasters, such as drought or floods, they tend to be chronic in areas where the normal margin between plenty and scarcity is precariously in the balance, in lands with limited carrying capacity and best suited for pastoral agriculture, such as in much of sub-Saharan Africa. They may smolder on for years, with little attention being paid to them either by the national governments involved or by the West, until sensational television coverage arouses acute interest. Under such circumstances, public concern in Western countries is likely to be faddish in nature and can be expected to fade away at least partially after a few weeks or months.

The African famine that has caused such terrible suffering over the last decade has affected a band of nearly thirty countries stretching across the continent from West to East. The drought that underlay the famine has resulted from a number of factors, including the widespread phenomenon of desertification—the southward movement of the Sahara desert. The spread of the desert in turn has resulted from a profound change in Africa's climate that appears to be related to the destruction of the rain forests through carelessness, greed, or ignorance. In 1983, for example, the Ivory Coast had its first recorded drought, with many fires in cocoa and coffee plantations resulting from the tinder-dry conditions. Careless and greedy exploitation of the forests in that country have nearly destroyed an irreplaceable natural resource. Coupled with this is the fact that grazing lands in sub-Saharan Africa suited only for low-intensity pastoral agriculture can be readily denuded of their grass cover by overgrazing.

Famines are much more complex in origin than a simple shortage of food. In almost every recorded famine, there has been food, often lots of it, in or near the famine area. In the Biafran famine in Nigeria in the late 1960s, landlords deliberately held back grain from the market in order to drive up prices. Thus it is invariably the poor who suffer most during a famine. In famine situations the very young, the infirm, and the very old are most vulnerable. They are unable to compete successfully for scanty supplies and get less than their share.

Deaths from starvation in Africa, as elsewhere, are almost invariably associated with social disruption and epidemics of infectious diseases. In famine situations, most people usually die from infectious disease rather than from starvation.

Famine relief efforts in Africa, if they are to get to the root of the problem, must be seen as long-term commitments. It will take many years to reestablish agricultural production and community life in the drought-scarred lands of Ethiopia, for example, even after the rains come back.

Planting cassava on Church welfare farm

The major responses to a food crisis in Africa originate with the African people themselves. Western media and governments tend to view food crises in Africa as dramatic, catastrophic events that spring full-blown on ignorant, unsuspecting people. Africans know better; they understand that a food crisis develops over an extended period of time and is not a single discrete event. For them, droughts and food shortages are chronic, long-term problems.

Far from being caught helplessly by the surprise of an unsuspected food shortage, African farmers and villagers have well-developed early-warning systems that alert them to the fact that a crisis is on its way. These include observations of natural phenomena and human behavior. The people concerned promptly bring into play a series of well-developed defense mechanisms, all designed to buffer or dampen the effects of the drought. Once the signs of an impending drought appear, rural families prepare for hard times by building up reserves of food stocks. Although African pastoralists are devoted to their flocks and herds, animals are sold for cash to buy food. The women play a crucial role in managing and conserving family food supplies. Cash, food, and hospitality are

53

exchanged between village dwellers, usually the hardest hit in a drought, and their extended families in the cities. These exchanges represent an expression of deeply held African beliefs in interdependence. Only when all else fails do large numbers of people migrate in search of food, either to the cities or across national boundaries.

The Church of Jesus Christ of Latter-day Saints has played a significant role in famine relief in Ethiopia. Church members in the United States and Canada held two special fasts for African relief at the request of the First Presidency in 1984–85 and contributed several millions of dollars to relief efforts. Over five million dollars were spent on food and on trucks to convey it. In addition, the Church has sponsored construction of a major irrigation project in northern Ethiopia, near the village of Goddobar, about 325 miles north of Addis Ababa, the capital.

Since this project represents a major attempt to carry out famine relief in the Lord's way by enhancing self-reliance, it is perhaps worthwhile to discuss it in some detail. The project involves a diversion weir on the Gambora River. The river is springfed and did not dry up even during the height of the 1981–84 drought. The weir, 28 meters long and 1.4 meters high, is constructed of concrete, with an apron of concrete about 35 meters deep in front of it. The weir, of course, does not stop the flow of all the water; it is not a dam. It checks the flow, which is diverted on either side into concrete pipes and then into twenty-four kilometers (fifteen miles) of irrigation canals. When fully completed, the project will provide irrigation water for about 400 hectares (960 acres) of land in a beautiful mountain valley. Involved are 1,640 farming families, numbering nearly 10,000 people. When I visited the site in December 1987, thirty to forty acres were already being irrigated as the project progressed, and bananas, guava, and some vegetables (onions, peppers, tomatoes) were being grown.

The project is exciting for a number of reasons. It incorporates basic gospel principles in its design and execution.

54

First, it permits the farmers to be self-reliant — to grow all the food they need, every year, regardless of whether it rains or not. Second, it is owned and will be operated by the farmers themselves. Their enthusiasm for it obviously is high. The operation and maintenance of the system involves very low-level technology. In the main, all that is needed is periodic dredging of the canals with a shovel to ensure they don't get clogged with silt. Finally, the farmers have built it themselves, under supervision of Africare[2] and Ethiopian Ministry of Agriculture engineers. All of the labor has been supplied locally. All twenty-four kilometers of irrigation canals have been dug by hand, with picks and shovels. The total work involved amounts to about 125,000 man days. Those who worked were paid with food — approximately one pound of grain per family member daily. Many of the men involved, who live in villages high in the mountains surrounding the valley farmland, left home at 5:30 A.M., walked two-and-a-half hours to the project site, worked ten-and-a-half hours, and then walked home again. The few skilled laborers, such as the concrete masons and the man operating the cement mixer, were paid in cash — approximately one dollar a day. They are all local residents who learned on the job. Workmanship is excellent.

In essence, what the project does is ensure the future, insofar as food is concerned, for 10,000 people in three villages. They and their children and their children's children will have the means, come what may in the way of rain, to grow the food they need and in greater amount and variety than ever before. There will be surplus food to sell. Furthermore, the Ethiopian government plans to establish a dairy cooperative in the valley next to the project, since irrigated pastures will be available for cattle to graze. A small dairy herd has already been established.

---

[2]Africare is a U.S.-based agency with extensive experience in developing aid projects in Africa.

The project has been lauded by the Ethiopian government as perhaps the best development project in the whole country. Fikre Silassie, the prime minister, has visited it, as have three vice ministers, the chief of the Relief and Reconstruction Commission, and assorted senior bureaucrats. All have praised it highly. "Why can we not get others to carry out similar projects, rather than spending vast amounts on that which does not bring self-reliance?" Mr. Silassie asked. The project has been featured three times on national TV in Ethiopia and has been visited by numerous international aid agencies. The government is using it as the model for other groups to follow.

In summary, Africans face temporal problems so serious that in the aggregate they suffer more than any other people on earth. Recently, Drs. Sharon L. Camp and J. Joseph Spiedel compiled the International Human Suffering Index, which was created to measure differences in living conditions between countries. (Population Crisis Committee, Washington, D.C., 1987.) Each individual country index is compiled by adding ten measures of human welfare: income, inflation, demands for new jobs, urban population pressures, infant mortality, nutrition, clean water, energy use, adult literacy, and personal freedom. Each of the ten measures of well-being was ranked from zero to ten, with the most distressful being ten. The values for each of the measures were then added together to give an overall human suffering index. Significantly, of the thirteen countries with the highest human suffering index, twelve were in Africa: Mozambique (the worst), Angola, Chad, Mali, Ghana, Somalia, Niger, Burkina Faso, Central African Republic, Zaire, Benin, and Malawi. Only one non-African country, Afghanistan, was found in the sixteen countries with the highest human suffering indices. There is no question about it: if the price of spiritual blessings be suffering and travail, our African brothers and sisters are well prepared to receive all that God hath prepared to bless His children.

CHAPTER FOUR

The Revelation on the Priesthood

The golden key that unlocked the door to bringing the fullness of the gospel to Black Africa was the revelation on priesthood, received in June 1978. That marvelous manifestation of God's love for all of His children in all ages and nations, of His Fatherhood over all the myriad of kindreds, tongues, and peoples on the earth, was in fulfillment of prophetic utterances long since delivered.

Nephi, son of Lehi, speaking of Jesus the Lord Omnipotent declared: "He doeth that which is good among the children of men; and he doeth nothing save it be plain unto the children of men; and he inviteth them all to come unto him and partake of his goodness; and he denieth none that come unto him, black and white, bond and free, male and female; and he remembereth the heathen; and all are alike unto God, both Jew and Gentile." (2 Nephi 26:33.)

Paul of Tarsus boldly affirmed on Mars Hill in Athens that "God that made the world and all things therein . . . hath made of one blood all nations of men for to dwell on all the face of the earth, and hath determined the times before appointed, and the bounds of their habitation." (Acts 17:24, 26.)

Later, writing to the Galatian saints, Paul reemphasized the great central truth that we are all God's children. Said he: "For as many of you as have been baptized into Christ have put on

Christ. There is neither Jew nor Greek, there is neither bond nor free, there is neither male nor female: for ye are all one in Christ Jesus. And if ye be Christ's, then are ye Abraham's seed, and heirs according to the promise." (Galatians 3:26–29.)

The revelation on priesthood must be seen against the background of the eternal mission of The Church of Jesus Christ of Latter-day Saints — to assist the Father and Son in their divine task of bringing to pass the "immortality and eternal life of man." (Moses 1:39.) The three aspects of that eternal mission may be expressed in a somewhat shorthand form as follows: to preach the gospel, to perfect the Saints, and to redeem the dead. The divine commandment to preach the gospel to all nations, given to us by the Savior Himself, was of course facilitated in Black Africa by the revelation. But the impact of the revelation is much more profound than that. To understand it fully, one must consider in somewhat greater detail the mission of the Church as articulated by the First Presidency and Quorum of the Twelve. That mission is as follows:

1. To proclaim the gospel of the Lord Jesus Christ to every nation, kindred, tongue, and people, to prepare them to receive the ordinances of baptism and confirmation as members of the Church.

2. To perfect the Saints by preparing them to receive the ordinances of the gospel and by instruction and discipline to gain exaltation.

3. To redeem the dead by performing vicarious ordinances of the gospel for those who have lived on the earth.

In these three aspects of the mission of the Church, note the importance placed on sacred ordinances and the holy covenants associated with them. Preaching the gospel and perfecting the Saints achieve purpose and direction only as we understand the central nature, the supernal importance, of ordinances and covenants. They prepare us in all things to be qualified to enter into the presence of the Lord. Those who administer the ordinances and covenants must be legal administrators, bearers of God's holy priesthood, who act with authority with the power to bless and bind — a power that extends beyond the veil of death into the eternities of time. (See Matthew 16:19.) Males who receive the ordinances of exaltation must have been ordained to the Melchizedek Priesthood — the holy priesthood that carries with it the power to govern with authority in the affairs of the kingdom of God.

Thus, the consummate cosmic significance of the revelation on priesthood to the peoples of Black Africa is that it provides the way for men, "called of God, by prophecy, and by the laying on of hands by those who are in authority, to . . . administer in the ordinances of the Gospel." (Article of Faith 5.) It permits the fullness of the gospel to be received and practiced with joy by our African brothers and sisters. It allows them to receive the supernal blessings of God's holy temple, with the sacred ordinances and associated covenants given only in the House of the Lord, including celestial marriage. Now our African brothers can preach and teach the gospel *with authority*, baptize *with authority*, bless their families *with authority*, administer in the ordinances of the gospel *with authority*, receive the blessings of the holy temple, and be prepared in all things to qualify them to return to the presence of the Lord. Because they are His authorized servants, they can receive divine assurance that their efforts to do the Lord's work are acknowledged and ratified by Him. Our African sisters likewise can partake in all of the blessings associated with the fullness of the glorious gospel of Christ.

A Glorious Experience

How was the revelation received? Out of a proper sense of propriety, a godly reluctance to speak too freely of sacred things, an unwillingness to expose sacred treasures to the vulgar gaze of sensation seekers, those who know the details have wisely declined to speak extensively about them. We do, how-

59

ever, know something of the general aspects of the process involved from the central earthly participant, President Spencer W. Kimball. In a talk at the institute of religion adjacent to the University of Utah, he explained:

> We had the glorious experience of having the Lord indicate clearly that the time had come when all worthy men and women everywhere can be fellowheirs and partakers of the full blessings of the gospel. I want you to know, as a special witness of the Savior, how close I have felt to him and to our Heavenly Father as I have made numerous visits to the upper rooms in the temple, going on some days several times by myself. The Lord made it very clear to me what was to be done. We do not expect the people of the world to understand such things, for they will always be quick to assign their own reasons or to discount the divine process of revelation. (*New Era,* April 1980, p. 36.)

In a newspaper interview, President Kimball reemphasized the searching and reaching and striving to understand the will of the Lord involved in the receipt of the revelation. "I went to the temple alone, day after day," he said, "and especially on Sundays and Saturdays when there were no organizations in the temple, when I could have it alone. This went on for some time as I was searching, because I wanted to be sure." (Quoted by Edward L. Kimball in *This People,* Summer 1988, p. 22.)

President Kimball's statements tell us much about the process involved in receiving revelation. A spiritual price must be paid. Deep, sustained spiritual effort is involved. Great faith and devotion are needed. Pleading, prayer, fasting, importuning, meditating, pondering, all may be required. Heaven knows how to place a proper price on her treasures, and yields them only to trusted servants.

Having taken the matter repeatedly to the Lord, the Prophet then took the final, momentous step in the Salt Lake Temple on June 1, 1978: "After we began to think of it seriously, we held a meeting of the Council of the Twelve in the temple on

Native missionaries
in Africa

the regular day and we considered this very seriously and thoughtfully and prayerfully. I offered the final prayer there and I told the Lord if it wasn't right, if He didn't want this change to come into the Church, that I would be true to it all the rest of my life and I'd fight the world against it. I would be loyal and true to the program if that's what He wanted. Then, as we had a special prayer circle, I knew that the time had come." (Ibid.)

It is apparent that President Kimball had not discussed with his family the intense spiritual struggle involved with receipt of the revelation. It was so sacred it demanded absolute privacy. Undoubtedly, if asked he would have reiterated the words of one of his noble counselors, President Marion G. Romney, who on one occasion said: "I do not tell all I know. I have not told my wife all I know. I have found that if I tell everything I know and explain every experience that I have had, the Lord will not trust me." (Quoted by Boyd K. Packer, Church Employees Lecture Series, January 18, 1980.)

Reference has been made to the pleading, importuning, faith, and humble supplication involved in receipt of the revelation on the priesthood. Another factor was also involved. God clearly has a divine timetable according to which nations and peoples and races are to be offered the saving, exalting truths of the gospel. It has always been so. Christ Himself took His gospel only to the house of Israel. Said He to the Twelve: "Go not into the way of the Gentiles, . . . but go rather to the lost sheep of the house of Israel." (Matthew 10:5-6.) It was only later, when the time was propitious, that the resurrected Lord commanded that the gospel should be preached "to every creature." (Mark 16:15.)

It is apparent from Paul's great sermon on Mars Hill (Acts 17) that he too understood there is a divine timetable, an appointed time, for peoples, races, and societies to be offered the full fruits of the gospel. There can be little doubt, therefore, that President Kimball's humble, pleading supplication came at that moment in history when the God of Heaven in His wisdom knew the time had come to offer the fullness of the glorious gospel, with all of its blessings and obligations, to His African children. In response to the pleading of the Prophet, God was prepared to open the celestial gates. The time had come for the dawning of a new day over Africa.

Other participants in the revelation have recorded some of their impressions of the process involved.

Elder Bruce R. McConkie bore his testimony of that sacred occasion as follows:

> The Spirit of the Lord rested mightily upon us all; we felt something akin to what happened on the day of Pentecost and at the dedication of the Kirtland Temple. From the midst of eternity, the voice of God, conveyed by the power of the Spirit, spoke to his prophet. The message was that the time had now come to offer the fulness of the everlasting gospel, including celestial marriage, and the priesthood, and the blessings of the temple, to all men, without reference to

race or color, solely on the basis of personal worthiness. And we all heard the same voice, received the same message, and became personal witnesses that the word received was the mind and will and voice of the Lord. . . .

In the days that followed the receipt of the new revelation, President Kimball and President Ezra Taft Benson—the senior and most spiritually experienced ones among us—both said, expressing the feelings of us all, that neither of them had ever experienced anything of such spiritual magnitude and power as was poured out upon the Presidency and the Twelve that day in the upper room in the house of the Lord. And of it I say: It is true; I was there; I heard the voice; and the Lord be praised that it has come to pass in our day. ("The New Revelation on Priesthood," in *Priesthood,* Salt Lake City, Deseret Book, 1981, p. 128.)

President Gordon B. Hinckley also was present that glorious day. In a talk given May 15, 1988, in a Churchwide fireside commemorating the restoration of the priesthood, he spoke movingly about the experience. Said he:

The Spirit of God was there. And by the power of the Holy Ghost there came to [President Kimball] an assurance that the thing for which he prayed was right, that the time had come, and that now the wondrous blessings of the priesthood should be extended to worthy men everywhere regardless of lineage. Every man in that circle, by the power of the Holy Ghost, knew the same thing. It was a quiet and sublime occasion. There was not the sound "as of a rushing mighty wind," there were not "cloven tongues like as of fire" (Acts 2:2–3) as there had been on the Day of Pentecost. But there was a Pentecostal spirit, for the Holy Ghost was present. No voice audible to our physical ears was heard. But the voice of the Spirit whispered with certainty into our minds and our very souls. (*Ensign,* October 1988, p. 70.)

From a careful reading of these accounts, it is apparent

THE DAWNING OF A BRIGHTER DAY

that the voice heard that day was the voice of the Spirit, inaudible to physical ears but indelibly imprinted in the minds and souls of those present. It was with them as with the Nephite prophet Enos, who recorded: "And while I was thus struggling in the spirit, behold, the voice of the Lord came into my mind." (Enos 1:10.) It is also clear that the event had a profound, lasting effect on all those involved. Said President Hinckley: "Not one of us who was present on that occasion was ever quite the same after that."

Reaction to the Revelation

Announcement of the revelation burst like a bombshell, not only on the Church but also on the world. Many of us can remember exactly where we were and what we were doing the day we first heard the announcement. It ranks in our memories with events such as the assassination of President John F. Kennedy; June 6, 1944, "D-Day" in Europe; or the explosion of the Challenger spacecraft.

For my part, I heard the announcement over the telephone from my stake president, and I recall being first incredulous and then weeping with joy and wonderment at the Lord's love for His children. That feeling of intense joy was widespread among Latter-day Saints worldwide, who, with few exceptions, accepted the revelation at once, in gratitude and thanksgiving.

The world, as could be expected, was more cynical about the revelation, although it received front-page coverage and lead-story prominence. Completely missing the point of it all, the New York *Times* termed the revelation "another example of the adaptation of Mormon beliefs to American culture." This erroneous view was echoed in many other media reports. Commenting on that view, Dr. Jan Shipps, associate professor of history and religious studies at Indiana University–Purdue University, and an influential and very knowledgeable observer of the Mormon scene, stated as follows:

Despite the seductive persuasiveness of this interpretation, the June 9 revelation will never be fully understood if it is regarded simply as a pragmatic doctrinal shift ultimately designed to bring Latter-day Saints into congruence with mainstream America. The timing and context, and even the wording of the revelation itself, indicate that the change has to do not with America so much as with the world. . . . The inspiration which led President Kimball and his counselors to spend many hours in the Upper Room of the Temple pleading long and earnestly for divine guidance did not stem from a messy situation with blacks picketing the Church's annual conference in Salt Lake City, but was "the expansion of the work of the Lord over the earth." Predicting the impact of the June 9 revelation on the growth pattern of the Church would be risky. But the fact that this revelation came in the context of worldwide evangelism rather than domestic politics or American social and cultural circumstances is yet another indication that Mormonism can no longer be regarded as a 19th century religio-cultural artifact and dismissed as a footnote to the story of American religion. Mormonism is here to stay. (Jan Shipps, "The Mormons: Looking Forward and Outward," *The Christian Century,* August 16–23, 1978, pp. 761–66.)

Professor Shipps, though not a Latter-day Saint, understands much about us, seeing in the Church the rise of a new world faith. In my view she consistently strives to treat the Church and its doctrines with fairness and respect. Her interpretation of the importance of the revelation is, I think, substantially correct. The revelation must be seen against the background of God's love for all of His children, for all are alike unto Him, and of the divine mission of the Church to bring the fullness of the gospel to every nation, kindred, tongue, and people. At this Saturday night of the world's history, God has "given the blessings of the gospel to the last group of laborers in the vineyard," to quote Elder McConkie. In one sense, then, the revelation marks the end of the beginning of the Restoration and the setting in place of all necessary prerequisites for the last great surge forward of the latter-day work preparatory to the Second Coming of the Savior. All is now in place for the stone "cut out of the mountain without hands" to roll forth and cover the whole earth as the waters cover the mighty deep. (See Daniel 2.)

The revelation certainly forced us to look again at the doctrines and practices of the Church and to reconsider them under the lens of new light and knowledge. With the sweet and gentle humility and meekness so characteristic of him, President Kimball — that great spiritual giant — explained: "I had a great deal to fight, of course, myself largely, because I had grown up with the thought that Negroes should not have the priesthood, and I was prepared to go all the rest of my life till my death and defend it as it was. But this revelation and assurance came to me so clearly that there was no question about it." (Quoted in *This People,* Summer 1988, p. 22.)

Elder McConkie put the doctrinal issues in context in the following words:

> There are statements in our literature by the early brethren that we have interpreted to mean that the Negroes would not receive the priesthood in mortality. I have said the same things, and people write me letters and say, "You said such and such, and how is it now that we do such and such?" And all I can say to that is that it is time disbelieving people repented and got in line and believed in a living, modern prophet. Forget everything that I have said, or what President Brigham Young or President George Q. Cannon or whosoever has said in days past, that is contrary to the present revelation. We spoke with a limited understanding and without the light and knowledge that now has come into the world.
>
> We get our truth and our light line upon line and precept upon precept. We have now had added a new flood of intelligence and light on this particular subject, and it erases all the darkness and all the views and all the thoughts of the past. They don't matter any more.

It doesn't make a particle of difference what anybody ever said about the Negro matter before the first day of June 1978. It is a new day and a new arrangement, and the Lord has now given the revelation that sheds light out into the world on this subject. (*Priesthood,* pp. 131–32.)

Praise be to God that the heavens are not closed; that new light and knowledge can burst forth from celestial realms; and that the light of the fullness of the gospel of Christ, like a beam of transcendent clarity and effulgent beauty, now shines majestic upon all of God's children, in every land.

CHAPTER FIVE

Dedicating Three Lands in West Africa

Elder Marvin J. Ashton, a member of the Quorum of the Twelve Apostles, and I set off on August 29, 1987, for West Africa. Elder Ashton's assignment from the First Presidency was to dedicate Zaire, Liberia, and the Ivory Coast for the preaching of the gospel. I was privileged to accompany him. It was a great thrill for me, loving Africa as I have for much of my adult life, to see the power of the priesthood mobilized to call blessings down on those countries. On a more personal level, it was a wonderful opportunity to get to know Elder Ashton, who has long been a hero of mine, and from whom I learned a great deal every day of our association.

Our first stop was in Kinshasa, the capital city of Zaire. It sprawls over dusty hills, with untold thousands of flowering bougainvilleas and flamboyants splashing their colors against a squalid background of tin roofs, open sewers, and deeply rutted roads. It was night when we arrived, and as we left the airport my senses were once again assailed by the pulsating melange of sounds, smells, and sights of African cities: roadside vendors huddled under the velvet blanket of darkness around a single, dim streetlight, laughter, music, voices crying in pain or ecstasy, dark figures drifting by like disembodied souls or standing solemnly by the roadside; and hanging over it all the pungent odors of sweat, heat, wood smoke, and dust.

Elder Ashton asked me to conduct the dedication ceremony, held early in the morning of August 30 in the garden
of the home of a local member, Michael Bowcutt, president
of the Binza Branch and an American employee at the U.S.
Embassy. I was thrilled to do so; it was a historic moment of
great spiritual significance. At Elder Ashton's request, I gave a
few introductory remarks as follows:

> This is a sacred and glorious occasion, as we meet
> under the protecting and sheltering canopy of the trees
> in this gentle garden, to carry out the Lord's business
> in this choice land. We meet in near obscurity, in the
> very infancy of the Church in Zaire, little noticed by
> the world but perfectly secure in the knowledge of
> who we are and in whose cause we serve. We are here
> on the Lord's errand. This action ushers in a new era
> in the history of the Church in Zaire. It is the dawning
> of a new day—a day whose beneficent influence will
> be felt through all generations of time. We who are
> mortal see countries and borders, tribes and peoples,
> but He who sees all knows only one people—one
> flock—all of whom are His children.
>
> My thoughts have turned this morning to the great
> hymn of the restoration composed by Parley P. Pratt,
> an early apostle of the Lord who was martyred for his
> beliefs. Wrote he: "The morning breaks, the shadows
> flee; lo, Zion's standard is unfurled! The dawning of a
> brighter day majestic rises on the world."
>
> How fitting those words are for this occasion, as we
> meet early in the morning of a majestic day. They tell
> us much about why we are here. They convey a sense
> of the great and glorious cause in which we all labor.
> They portray in poetic language the most important
> truth in the world—that the gospel of Christ has again
> been restored to the earth in all of its fullness; that it
> has burst upon the scene like a light of transcendent
> brightness, dispelling the long night of spiritual dark-
> ness which covered the world for so many years; caus-
> ing the shadows of error to flee and the dawn of a new

69

and glorious day to break resplendent upon all countries and peoples.

Ours is the responsibility, as the bearers of God's priesthood and His authority, to bring that glorious message to all the world. The message we bring is one of joy and hope. It speaks of prophets and revelation. It proclaims that the heavens are not closed. Its central figure is the Christ. It tells of His atoning sacrifice which opens the way for each of us to return to our Father's house, on condition of faithfulness.

This is our message to the world, and we will not rest until it has penetrated every continent, been preached in every clime, and sounded in every ear. Come, we say to all of God's children. Come sup at the table of the Lord. Come learn of Him. Come and partake of sacred ordinances and covenants which will enable you, if you remain faithful, to taste the sweet joys of your Heavenly Father's kingdom. Come listen to a prophet's voice and hear the words of God.

The dedicatory prayer offered by Elder Ashton was short, quiet, and spiritually powerful, delivered with great eloquence and sincerity. Here are some excerpts from his remarks:

O God, our Eternal and Heavenly Father, unitedly on this beautiful morning we assemble with bowed heads and thankful hearts. By appointment of the First Presidency and the Council of the Twelve Apostles, I now humbly exercise the authority of the holy apostleship and dedicate and bless this great land of Zaire to Thee and Thy purposes for the sharing of the gospel of Jesus Christ in its fullness. May The Church of Jesus Christ of Latter-day Saints now roll forward according to Thy will and eternal plans with rapidity and permanence.

Heavenly Father, we thank Thee for this historical situation. We express sincere appreciation for friendly government officials for signing a document giving the Church legal authority to continue our missionary efforts among these choice people. We are also grateful to full-time missionaries whose labors and commitment have been an important element in this day's significant recognition.

May those who live, labor, and lead in this choice country, which is ripe for the gospel, find joy in their labors. May all of us who relate to and serve in this country proclaim with excitement and anxiousness the reality that the gospel of Jesus Christ has been restored in its fullness through the Prophet Joseph Smith and is now available to all of God's children. Almighty God, inspire and lead our missionaries to teach and baptize individuals and families — not groups or tribes during this season of time.

Heavenly Father, we thank Thee for this great nation and these God-fearing and spiritually sensitive people. We pray that in the days to come great multitudes will enjoy the priceless gifts available to those who embrace and live the true gospel of Thy Son, Jesus Christ. May Thy earthly kingdom roll forward now in Zaire with stability, love, and eternal purpose.

Our next stop was Monrovia, the capital of Liberia. Elder Ashton's prayer as he dedicated that country thrilled all who heard it, with its rich eloquence and deep spirituality. As I listened, choked with emotion, it seemed to me that the God of Heaven must have been pleased indeed as He looked down upon His apostle-son. I sensed that the humble yet authoritative use of priesthood power was fully acceptable to our Heavenly Father.

Excerpts from the text of Elder Ashton's prayer include the following:

Our Eternal Heavenly Father, we are humbly grateful this day to meet and be about Thy business. Joy is in our hearts as we contemplate the privilege of going into this part of the world for sacred and eternal purposes. By appointment from the First Presidency and the Council of the Twelve Apostles, we dedicate this land of Liberia to Thee and Thy purposes. May The Church of Jesus Christ of Latter-day Saints grow steadily under Thy influence and power from this important date

71

LDS meetinghouse in Ikat Ekong, Nigeria

onward. May those here today and others who will follow proclaim the gospel with anxiousness and commitment. May they and those they lead be perfected by sharing and living the truths of the gospel.

Heavenly Father, we bless this land of Liberia. May peace and stability reign so Thy work will prosper. We thank those who have labored and cooperated to give the Church legal authority to continue our missionary efforts. Help us to live and labor in the spirit of love with all mankind. Keep Thy servants free of contention and pride. Impress us to be understanding and patient under all circumstances. Frustrate those who would impede or slander our effort.

Bless the honest in heart in this country. Bless Thy children, to be responsive to Thy truths and the glorious messages of Thy Son, Jesus Christ. May the fields be ripe and ready for the harvest. Help us to thrust in our sickles with friendly and strong arms. We thank Thee for the knowledge we share that souls brought unto Thee will bring joy.

That evening we attended a meeting of local members of

the New Cru Town Branch in an old ramshackle building that had at one time served as a cinema. Through its cracked and crumbling walls came the steady beat of African street sounds — the chatter of vendors, the blare of a radio, a child's strident cry, a raucous laugh. Yet the Spirit was there in its richness, and hearts were lifted and edified by Elder Ashton's message of hope and faith. At the end of the meeting both Elder Ashton and I were presented with Liberian native costumes, richly decorated gowns and hats in vivid colors. When we modeled them for the crowd, they clapped and cheered in great good humor. Given the poverty of the members, we appreciated that we had received royal gifts.

The final leg of our journey took us to Abidjan, the capital city of Ivory Coast and aptly named the Paris of Africa. As had been our custom, we met to dedicate the land in the quiet garden of a local member family. Elder Ashton, with the eloquence and power to which I had become accustomed, again poured out his heart to his Heavenly Father. Said he:

> Heavenly Father, humbly we approach Thy heavenly throne with joyous hearts. This is a day of great importance for this land, its people, and the future. Hear our prayers and accept our gratitude as we share the feelings of our hearts. We dedicate this land of Ivory Coast for the preaching of the gospel and for all of Thy purposes. Hasten the day, our Father, when Thy work will go forward as a powerful stone rolling forward on Thy decreed course. Bless those who have prayed and labored for this day and its significance. We pray for the leaders of this nation. Bless them with Thy spirit as they lead, serve, and plan. May peace and love form a proper foundation for The Church of Jesus Christ of Latter-day Saints to grow, prosper, and lift lives unto Thee. This nation, soil, and people are Thine. We pray for Thy assistance as we now labor to share the truth in Thine own way.

The Lord's errand was complete. Three great lands had

been dedicated to Him, that His glorious work might roll forth with power and majesty to bless the lives of millions. On a more personal basis it was thrilling to sit at the feet of an apostle, to feel his mighty faith and marvel at his humble prayers of dedication. Elder Ashton is one of the Lord's great sons. He doesn't take himself too seriously, but he is in no doubt at all about who called him nor whose authority he bears. He will ever be one of my role models, and I shall never forget those glorious days when I was privileged to assist him "on the Lord's errand."

CHAPTER SIX

Nigeria: The Black Giant
of Africa

Each time I thread my way through the chaos, inefficiency, heat, and bedlam of the airport at Lagos, Nigeria, I find myself wondering if I'll ever make it in one piece and asking myself why I ever left home. Nonetheless, after each visit to Nigeria I feel a warm glow of satisfaction and intense exhilaration. I realize I've been in the most exciting country in Black Africa — a country that pulsates with a beat louder and faster than that of any other on the continent, populated by a people who are exuberant, boisterous, argumentative, and in a hurry. They push, shove, and bicker on the streets, refusing to queue up quietly as do their less combative neighbors in other African countries. Line-ups of motorists at a gasoline station in Lagos not uncommonly degenerate into fisticuffs, as some impatient soul tries to push to the head of the line and is immediately challenged by those already there.

Perhaps one reason why Nigerians are so self-assertive and boisterous is that the country has a long and distinguished history and culture and much to be proud of. Its northern cities, such as Kano, were sophisticated southern anchors on the trans-Saharan caravan routes one thousand years ago. As mentioned previously, when Europeans visited Benin in the fifteenth century, they found a highly organized and advanced people whose artisans produced in ivory, bronze, terra-cotta,

75

and brass works that are recognized today throughout the world as masterpieces.

By all counts, Nigeria is the most important country in Black Africa. Probably one-quarter of all Africans are Nigerian. Although no one knows for certain, since a full census of the country has not been taken since independence in 1960, there are somewhere between 90 million and 110 million inhabitants, more than any country in Western Europe. Nor is Nigeria an economic pygmy. The gross domestic product exceeds that of South Africa, with all of its gold and diamonds, and is more than 50 percent that of all other forty-five sub-Saharan countries of Africa combined.

The country is a melange of over two hundred ethnic groups and many dozens of different languages, but there are three major tribes, which are actually small nations. They include the Hausa and Fulani of northern Nigeria, Islamic people with Arab ties who are great horsemen and whose tribal kings built crenellated palaces of baked mud; the self-confident and entrepreneurial Yoruba in the West; and the Ibos of eastern Nigeria, who under the patronage of the British colonial government became the administrators, educators, and businessmen—the backbone of bureaucracy and commerce in the country. The three major tribes live together in an uneasy union made more complicated and tentative by religious tension between the Muslim north and the Christian-animist south.

Geographically, Nigeria also presents a vast panorama of contrasts. The size of Arizona, Utah, and California combined, its landmass is approximately one-tenth that of the United States. The southern coast, along the Gulf of Guinea, is dominated by mangrove swamps, which give way to rain forest farther inland, with trees reaching as high as 200 feet. The central plateau is characterized by wooded savanna, with the vegetation becoming increasingly sparse as one travels farther north. The northern part of the country is barren, desolate desert, its arid surface swept by the harmattan, the hot, dry wind from the Sahara.

Lagos, the capital, is a sprawling, lusty giant of a place. Its streets are dirty, though less so than a decade ago when they were just plain filthy. In those days uncollected and rotting garbage lay in heaps on every street, and the air from the airport to the city was filled with the acrid smoke from burning tires and smoldering heaps of rancid refuse. To be caught in a traffic jam in Lagos, called a "go-slow" by the locals, is still an exercise in patience and forbearance that at times can be well nigh intolerable. Traveling the thirteen miles from the Lagos airport to the city can take as long as several hours. What redeems the place, in spite of the open sewers, congestion, and squalid slums, is the feeling of excitement in the air — the sense that what happens there really matters, not only in Nigeria, but far beyond its borders; a realization that this is a country that sets the pace for the rest of Black Africa.

The major problem with Lagos is that it simply has grown too fast, from 300,000 to well over three million inhabitants in just a decade, as people from all over the country have crowded into its festering slums seeking a better life than that to be found in subsistence agriculture in rural areas. Indeed, greater Lagos probably has a population exceeding ten million people. The physical infrastructures needed for life support — water, sewerage, electricity, street services — have been overwhelmed, as the city and its environs sink under their own weight.

Other smaller cities in the country are far less congested and the pace there is far less hectic. One of my favorites is Enugu, the old British capital of eastern Nigeria. There one finds broad, tree-lined boulevards, neat whitewashed houses, a good hotel, flowers, and grass. The air is crisp and cool on the eastern plateau, and darkness comes softly and gently, drawing a velvet blanket over the sleeping city. It is a lovely place.

77

Traveling on Nigerian roads can be a devastating experience, particularly for uninitiated Americans or Europeans used to high standards of road safety and relatively courteous drivers. According to an article in the highly respected magazine *West Africa* (August 22, 1988), in the past decade more than 400,000 serious road accidents were recorded in Nigeria, and more than 100,000 people died on the roads. These grim statistics have earned Nigeria the dubious reputation of having the worst road-accident record in the world.

There are many reasons for the carnage on Nigerian highways. For one thing, most roads are in terrible states of repair, and road maintenance is practically nonexistent. At times, many sections of the highway linking Lagos with the eastern parts of the country look as though the road had been strafed from the air. The road surface is pitted and broken, with gaping potholes that can rupture tires and rip off fuel tanks of cars with unwary drivers. In mid-1988, a long segment of the road was washed away by floods and became, in the words of an editorial in one of the Nigerian newspapers, "a veritable death-trap."

Apart from lack of adequate road infrastructure and road maintenance, bad driving causes many accidents. Nigerian drivers, almost all of whom are men, use the automobile to express publicly their machismo tendencies. Speeding, cutting in on other drivers, and a general lack of care and caution, coupled with get-out-of-my-way aggressiveness, characterize the driving habits of the majority. A common scene on a Nigerian highway is a long line of automobiles creeping along at a snail's pace behind a long-distance heavy transport truck, which plods along, taking its half of the road down the middle. Sooner or later one of the frustrated motorists, perhaps a taxi driver with a dilapidated, grossly overloaded car, pulls out to pass, right into the path of an oncoming vehicle. Multiple injuries and often multiple deaths ensue. A dozen or more passengers often are packed like sardines into a minivan, some even hanging onto the outside of the vehicle. Under such circumstances, a crash can only result in disaster.

After a road accident, corpses often lay on or at the side of the road for several days before being identified. In November 1988 I passed a corpse that had lain unclaimed for over a week on the road between Ibadan and Benin City, a gruesome reminder of one of the harsh realities of African life.

Bodies may be taken to mortuaries in different hospitals, and the injured may be admitted to hospitals or clinics scattered over a wide area. Since records are not kept, or are sketchy and inaccurate at best, finding a patient or receiving the body of a victim becomes a nightmare.

What does all of this mean for missionaries and other expatriates living in Nigeria? The answer is: be alert, drive defensively but boldly, stay cool (don't duel with another driver for the right to be first), and be certain your vehicle is in top mechanical condition at all times. If these precautions are taken, one need not be unduly concerned about driving in Nigeria.

Another of the frustrations endemic to life in Nigeria is frequent interruptions in electric power, which have led to the Nigerian Electric Power Authority (NEPA) acquiring for its acronym the novel translation of Never Expect Power Always. Cynics proclaim that NEPA treats both high and low equally, supplying all with darkness more than light. As reported in the magazine *West Africa* (September 22, 1988), during a state banquet for the Ghanaian leader Jerry Rawlings in the northern Nigerian city of Kano in early 1988, NEPA broke down on two occasions, to the intense embarrassment of the Nigerian officials present. NEPA offers numerous excuses for its poor performance, ranging from the low level of power generation and inadequate staff discipline and training to the novel explanation of snakes taking over its transformers.

The same issue of *West Africa* reported on another of the problems faced by Nigerians as they try to move the country into the modern world. As of the end of September 1988, the waiting list of people wishing to have a telephone installed by the national telephone agency, Nitel, stretched to over 200,000, but only 33,000 will be lucky enough to get connected. Many attempt to override the list by bribing Nitel officials, and cries of corruption are heard on all sides. Among other problems, Nitel has to contend with the theft of telephone cables, the metal from which is used in making jewelry. In January 1988, 2,000 lines worth 3 million Naira (then about 400,000 U.S. dollars) were stolen in Lagos, and on one occasion Lagos Island was temporarily cut off from the world when thieves stole six cables located under a bridge.

British Rule and Independence

Nigeria fell under British influence late in the nineteenth century, and the British government assumed control of the country from the Royal Niger Company in 1900. (The company took its name from the mighty Niger, or "black," river that divides the country roughly from north to south.) In an attempt to develop a truly black colony, the British would not allow a white man to enter Nigeria, much less stay there, unless he could show good reason why he needed to do so.

In the early days, life for the British colonial administrators in Nigeria was very difficult. Not without reason was West Africa known as the white man's graveyard. The story of Sylvia Leith-Ross, a young Englishwoman who went to Nigeria with her husband and three other Britons in the late summer of 1907, illustrates some of the problems involved. Her husband was a government official, assigned to the British headquarters of northern Nigeria at that time, at a place called Zungeru. Said she, "I remember that we had to take absolutely everything with us, all clothing . . . all food and almost all furniture. But the bulk of our luggage consisted I suppose of the . . . boxes containing food for eighteen months. Mosquito nets, of course, had to be used everywhere and it was quite fatal not to do so."

Mrs. Leith-Ross and her husband had been in Zungeru for only a year when tragedy struck. She wrote:

> My husband had had blackwater [probably tertiary, or malignant, malaria] once before and had somehow survived, although he'd been completely alone. The second time it happened in Zungeru; one doesn't know why, it was just an infection, but at the time there was no known cure. He was at once taken to the small hospital and two doctors stayed with him day and night for two days, but he grew weaker and weaker and died within three days.
>
> Of course, death was accepted as part of the day's work, but he had been so much liked that the whole of his colleagues and even the black clerks and the transport boys were all shocked deeply and were, in a way, not so sorry for me as sorry for themselves in that they'd lost a friend and an example. Everybody was kindness itself to me but the only thing to do was for me to go home. And when I left I found that of the five of us who had started for Northern Nigeria, I was the only one to return to England. The others were all dead. (In Charles Allen, editor, *Tales from the Dark Continent*, London: Futura Publications, 1980, p. 38.)

Interestingly enough, Sylvia Leith-Ross went back to Nigeria, "for it was only when she [Nigeria] had done her worst that I realized how much I loved her." She became one of the early pioneers in the study of the Fulani language and culture and Nigeria's first female superintendent of education.

By the end of World War II, Nigeria was well on the way to independence, with a small but growing middle class, an elected parliament, an active and at times outspoken press, and a healthy agricultural sector that produced sufficient food to feed the people. At independence in 1960, the future of the country looked promising indeed, particularly in light of the discovery of oil in the Niger delta. Since then, however, there have been a terrible civil war and several *coups d'états*, as yesterday's promises have foundered on the rocks of corruption and inefficiency. At least some of the problem can be traced to the discovery and exploitation of oil, which in the view of many Nigerians has provided as many curses as blessings to the people. Get-rich-quick schemes, profiteering, massive corruption, and unrealistic pipe dreams of never-ending wealth have combined to shatter the hopes for a better tomorrow for millions of Nigerians. Despite it all, however, the country is struggling upward.

Perhaps the most promising sign that Nigeria can succeed in a modern world is the continued growth of the middle class. Students of history will no doubt recall that it was the birth of the middle class four centuries ago that enabled Britain and other European powers to develop the managerial infrastructures necessary for them to emerge as stable and powerful modern nations. The middle class provides the professional persons — physicians, lawyers, business leaders, bureaucrats, educators, and so forth — necessary to run a modern state. Its taxes fuel the machinery of government and its efforts generate the economic power needed for a modern country to run. Perhaps more importantly, it is from the middle class that The Church of Jesus Christ of Latter-day Saints is finding the leadership seedstock that represents a precious resource essential for the future growth of the Church in Nigeria.

Early Church Efforts

For two decades or more before the revelation on the priesthood was received in 1978, letters had come to Church headquarters in Salt Lake City from Christian Africans asking for "holy books" and information about the Church. Many of the letters came from Nigeria. Most of those who wrote knew little about the Church, but, impelled by the Spirit, they knew somehow that they needed to know more. Missionary pamphlets and tracts, which found their way into Africa by various means, were read and reread. Many who read them were touched by the Spirit and recognized that they had come across a great treasure, a pearl of great price. Others heard of the Church by word of mouth, from a brother, cousin, or friend who had studied in the United States or elsewhere. They too pondered, prayed, and believed.

Slowly, spontaneously, a miracle began to unfold. Independent of one another and without knowledge of the others' actions, several groups of humble African truth seekers in Nigeria began to organize themselves into churches. They built small meetinghouses and patterned their meetings, doctrine, organization, and even names after The Church of Jesus Christ of Latter-day Saints, as best they knew it. Since they lacked priesthood authority for what they were doing, there inevitably were errors and omissions in their actions, and they were Latter-day Saints in name only. Yet they sought the truth, were for the most part humble and sincere, and prayed for the day when missionaries would come among them with full authority to preach and baptize.

The Church was not unaware of what was happening in Nigeria and elsewhere in West Africa. On more than one occasion representatives were sent to appraise the situation and report to the First Presidency. On his way home from serving as president of the South African Mission, Glen G. Fisher of Cardston, Alberta, Canada, was asked by Church authorities in 1960 to stop in Lagos and investigate matters there. His unpublished account of that visit includes the following:

> On arrival [in Lagos] I found it most difficult to locate the people I wanted to see. The postmaster directed me to three churches, where he said I might find the man I was seeking. [At] the first church I visited I found four men seated on a verandah in front of the building. They were deep in discussion and did not see me until I stepped from the sidewalk onto the verandah. They immediately arose and came over to where I was standing. I introduced myself as a Mormon missionary and they immediately reached out and took both my hands. Never have I received a more sincere and enthusiastic

welcome. They led me to a chair and for three hours we sat and discussed the teachings of the Church.

A visit to their churches convinced me that members of the congregation were living in extreme poverty. In one church particularly I noted there were no seats, no musical instruments, and no pulpit. The leader of the group carried his supplies in a wooden box which he used as a pulpit. Supplies consisted of a few Bibles, some missionary pamphlets, the *Articles of Faith* by James E. Talmage, and *A Marvelous Work and a Wonder* by LeGrand Richards. This same literature I found in all of the churches I visited. There was also a copy of the Book of Mormon in one of the churches. From this literature a church organization had been effected, patterned after the Mormon church.

I discovered that for a number of years past they had been preparing their congregation for baptism into The Church of Jesus Christ of Latter-day Saints. Their president told me that they had two congregations with a total membership of over a thousand people, and with some pride he declared that not a single one either smoked or used alcoholic beverages. The members also paid tithing and they had been able to accumulate sufficient funds to erect two small chapels. (Letter from Glen G. Fisher to S. C. Brewerton, M. D., dated July 16, 1984; copy in possession of the author.)

President N. Eldon Tanner, first counselor in the First Presidency, LaMar Williams, who had served as secretary to the Missionary Department, and Ralph Walker of Calgary, Alberta, visited Nigeria on separate occasions a few years later for first-hand examinations of the situation, but problems in securing visas prevented representatives being sent to officially establish the Church there. The civil war in Nigeria (the so-called Biafra war) also made the situation more complex.

In August 1978, however, Edwin Q. ("Ted") Cannon, Jr., and Merrill Bateman of the Brigham Young University faculty were sent by the Church on a fact-finding tour of the groups in Nigeria and Ghana. They returned with the recommendation

Nigerian converts walk to river site for baptisms

that the Church move ahead in West Africa. Within months action was taken by Church officials. On November 8, 1978, two couples—Elder Rendell N. Mabey and his wife, Rachel, and Elder Cannon and his wife, Janath—were assigned to Nigeria as special representatives of the International Mission. With their arrival, the restored gospel of Christ began to take root in Nigeria.

During the year they labored in Nigeria and Ghana, the Cannons and Mabeys had much to do. Practices not in accordance with Church standards, including use of collection plates, and dancing, drumming, and pentecostal hallelujahs in church meetings had to be stopped and replaced with those which are fully acceptable to the Lord. The principles behind the practices had to be taught. The gospel had to be preached in power and purity. Baptisms had to be conducted by one who held the authority from God to do so. Yet the people were teachable and humble, and the Church grew. Brother Mabey has recorded the experiences of that great opening year in his book *Brother to Brother* (Salt Lake City: Bookcraft, 1982).

85

What a great debt we owe to those early stalwart pioneers who went forth boldly encountering situations and solving problems for which we as a church had no previous experience to guide them. They were led by the Spirit in their pioneering efforts and laid the groundwork for a mighty work.

The West Africa Mission, comprising the countries of Nigeria and Ghana, was formally created on April 1, 1980, under the direction of President Bryan Espenschied of Salt Lake City. He was succeeded in 1982 by President Sylvester Cooper of Rexburg, Idaho, who labored hard to strengthen the priesthood base. All members baptized earlier were laboriously retaught the discussions in their own language by specially trained Nigerian district missionaries. The need to modulate growth was recognized by bringing new members into the Church only as trained local priesthood leadership was available to assimilate and look after them properly. Several meetinghouses were built and other sites selected. The need to build the Church in Nigeria on solid gospel principles was reemphasized by succeeding mission presidents J. Duffy Palmer (1984–86), a retired Utah judge, and Robert E. Sackley (1986–88), now a General Authority.

In the early days of the Church in Nigeria most Church membership was concentrated in the southeastern part of the country, primarily in Cross River and Imo states. Many members were villagers engaged in subsistence agriculture, and more than a few were illiterate. Particularly under President Sackley's direction, the Church began to spread north and west, to open up missionary work among the inhabitants of the large cities of central and western Nigeria. Experience had taught us that large numbers of educated and employed people were to be found there, and that many were anxious to hear the gospel message. Furthermore, the weakening of the shackles of tribalism in the cities enables the gospel message to fall on more receptive ground therein.

Members of Nigerian branch enjoy activity

Leadership and Growth in 1989

By late 1989 there were nearly 13,000 members of the Church in Nigeria in nine districts — three districts in the Lagos Mission and six districts in the Aba Mission — and the Aba Nigeria Stake. Here is a brief rundown of the type of leadership found in the districts and branches at the time this book is being written, in 1989.

The Lagos District is headed by George Afful, an architect, who is an Ghanaian, baptized in Nigeria. Like President Afful, many Church members in Lagos are not Nigerians but have come from other African countries, principally Ghana, to seek work.

The Ibadan District president, Olisogon Akanbi, is a professor of engineering at the University of Ibadan. He is the first member of the Yoruba tribe to join the Church. His wife, also a Church member, was in the United Kingdom in late 1988, completing a graduate degree in business. At the end of 1989 there were several hundred members in Ibadan, in branches formed only a few months previously.

The Benin District, with approximately one thousand members in late 1989, had at that time several rented buildings and a recently constructed district center. The district president, John Ehanire, is the chief medical officer at the University of

Benin. He has a charming English wife and three sons, two of whom are attending a university in Nigeria.

In the Aba Mission, a new district was recently established in Onitsha, the great port on the Niger River. President of the district, which has several hundred members, is Patrick Ojaidi, an accountant.

The president of the Enugu District is Dr. Ike Ikeme, formerly a professor of food science at the University of Nigeria at Nsukka and currently employed by the Church Educational System. This district was formed in mid-1988, and by September of that year, it had over two hundred members, many of whom were associated with the university.

The Owerri District contains the Aboh Mbaise Branch, one of the first branches in the country. The district president, Judo Impney, a man of great stature and dignity, is a retired Nigerian public servant, now employed by the Church. He and his wife have nine children.

Chris Chukwurah, president of the Uyo District, has graduate degrees from two universities in the United States and is a professional educator employed by the Church as regional director of temporal affairs in Nigeria. Sister Chukwurah has a nursing degree and teaches nursing in a local college. I recall with pleasure being in their home a few days before Christmas in 1987 and listening to their tape recorder, with Bing Crosby singing "I'm Dreaming of a White Christmas." Since the temperature at the time was nearly 100 degrees F, it could only be a dream! President Chukwurah is a member of the Ibo tribe, presiding over a district of the Church containing a very high proportion of members from the Efik tribe.

The Etinan District, with nine units (six of which are housed in Church-owned buildings), is headed by Mbong Ifah Mbong, a school principal and university graduate. The majority of members in the district are farmers.

The Ikot Ikong District had approximately two thousand members in late 1989. Four of the buildings in the district are

African Saints make special presentation to Elder Alexander B. Morrison of the Second Quorum of the Seventy after a conference meeting

owned by the Church. The president, Donatus W. Ekwere, is a farmer, as are most Church members in the area.

The Calabar District is headed by Dr. Sunday Okore, a Brigham Young University graduate, who is a professor at the University of Calabar.

A Stake in Nigeria

Just as June 9, 1978, the day the revelation on the priesthood was announced, is a red-letter day in the history of the Church in Black Africa, so too must the date of May 15, 1988, stand as a milestone for all time. On that day, Elder Neal A. Maxwell of the Quorum of the Twelve, assisted by Elder Robert E. Sackley of the Second Quorum of the Seventy, created the Aba Nigeria Stake. This stake is not only the first in West Africa, but also the first in the history of the Church in which all leaders are blacks. In fact, *all* members of the stake are Africans.

Musing about the historic occasion, Elder Sackley spoke words that undoubtedly were in the hearts of many that day: "I have a feeling a great prophet is looking down upon us and smiling. The Lord obviously made it known to President Kimball that the day had come."

More than a thousand of the stake's 2,300 members crowded into the Aba meetinghouse to listen to one of the Savior's special witnesses speak of divinely inspired timing and planning that had culminated in the formation of a stake. As reported in *Church News,* May 21, 1988, Elder Maxwell quoted Alma 29:8: "For behold, the Lord doth grant unto all nations, of their own nation and tongue, to teach his word, yea, in wisdom, all that he seeth fit that they should have." With the creation of the Aba Stake, he noted, "for this nation there now comes more of the gospel's fullness in the unfolding plan of the Lord."

Tears were shed as Elder Maxwell recounted how he had been present in the upper room of the temple that early June day in 1978 when the General Authorities gathered to receive the revelation and decision from President Spencer W. Kimball. "I wept with joy that day," Elder Maxwell said. "The handkerchief I wiped my tears with I took home and told my wife not to wash it. I put it in my book of remembrance, still bearing the marks of my tears of joy. On this Sunday, I have a second handkerchief that has wiped tears of joy. I will take it home and place it in my book of remembrance next to the other handkerchief."

Three outstanding young priesthood holders were sustained as the presidency of the new stake. David W. Eka, the stake president, has a master's degree in petroleum engineering from a British university and works for a large multinational oil company. His wife, Ekaete, also has a master's degree from a British university, in business administration. Ephraim S. Etete, the first counselor, is deputy superintendent of police in River State and will soon be the youngest police superintendent in Nigeria. Lazarus Onitchi, the second counselor, is an insurance company executive. On October 25, 1988, I had the privilege of witnessing the sealing of David and Ekaete Eka

Elder Robert L. Sackley of the Second Quorum of the Seventy, Brother and Sister Judo Impney of Nigeria, and Sister Sackley

in the London Temple. They were amazed, when they came into the sealing room, to encounter many friends there to witness that glorious event. As they knelt at the sacred altar, with Elder Neal A. Maxwell conducting the sealing ceremony, in my mind's eye I saw not only a beautiful young couple but a whole people, rising up in truth and righteousness to accept the fullness of the gospel of Christ. I saw them coming, now in a trickle, but soon in a flood, to receive the supernal blessings of the temple. And I saw the birth of a continent into the kingdom of God.

At its formation the new Aba Stake had six wards and three branches. Seven of the units met in Church-owned buildings. Of those, all but one were built by the Church, using a standard plan developed for use in Nigeria and admirably suited to the needs and conditions in the country.

At the time of its organization, the Aba Stake had more than three hundred Melchizedek Priesthood bearers, almost all of whom were active. Statistics for sacrament meeting attendance, home and visiting teaching, and other activities were fully comparable to those in stakes elsewhere in the world. Elder Sackley's remarks concerning Nigerian members in general certainly apply to those in the Aba Stake: "These are an intelligent people; many members are educated. I see some of the most capable leadership in Nigeria that could be found almost anywhere in the Church. Some of our members here are medical doctors, university professors and businessmen, as well as farmers and laborers. Some members not only have attended colleges but also have more than one degree. Many women in the Church have bachelor's and master's degrees."

In December 1988, I was privileged to attend the first semiannual conference of the Aba Stake. More than four hundred Melchizedek Priesthood bearers were present, and an additional 131 men were advanced to the Melchizedek Priesthood. Said President David Eka, "I prayed over each one of the names, to ensure God's approval before proceeding." The talks, prayers, and singing at all sessions of the conference were excellent, and the Spirit was felt in rich abundance by all who attended.

Six weeks after the formation of the new stake, on July 1, 1988, the First Presidency announced creation of a second mission in Nigeria, formed by a division of the Nigeria Lagos Mission. Within the new mission, called the Nigeria Aba Mission, are approximately forty million people in eastern Nigeria. Arthur W. Elrey, a retired mental health center administrator from Tucson, Arizona, was called as the first president of the mission. At the time of his call, he and his wife, Glena, were serving as missionaries in Nigeria. Unfortunately, in late 1988 Sister Elrey contracted a serious case of drug-resistant malaria, and she and her husband had to leave Nigeria. Joseph Grigg, an insurance executive from California, was called to succeed President Elrey, with his wife, Joan, serving by his side.

Richard D. Mathews of Logan, Utah, was called to replace Robert E. Sackley as president of the Nigeria Lagos Mission. He and his wife, Fay, had recently been released as temple missionaries in the Manila Philippines Temple. President Mathews, a retired oil company exploration manager, had previously lived in Nigeria with his family in connection with his employment.

Finding a "Lost Lamb"

In Nigeria, as elsewhere in developing countries, mission presidents are constantly on the alert for individuals who have been baptized elsewhere and have moved to remote locations far away from organized units of the Church. When these "lost lambs" eventually are located, they often know little about the Church, having forgotten much of what once was dear to them. Sad to say, a few perhaps do not really want to be found. Having lost their grip on the iron rod, they fall away into the dark abyss of sin and rebellion. Not infrequently, however, a noble soul is found — one who is anxious to enjoy the sweet fruits of fellowship with the Saints and who welcomes our emissaries with open heart and open arms. The following story is about one such noble soul.

In late 1987, Robert E. Sackley, then president of the Nigeria Lagos Mission, felt that the time had come to move the Church north and west from its center of strength in the eastern states of Imo and Cross River. One of the cities he decided to open was Enugu, the former British capital of eastern Nigeria. He felt certain that among the inhabitants of that lovely place were the elect of God, waiting to be taught the gospel.

About forty miles north of Enugu is the city of Nsukka, where the home campus of the University of Nigeria is located. President Sackley had heard that a professor at the university had been affiliated with the Church in America. He even had the man's name: Dr. Ike Ikeme, a Nigerian who had received a doctorate in food science in 1981 at Purdue University in Indiana. One of the great shepherds of the Church, President Sackley resolved to try to locate Professor Ikeme. He had a strange feeling about the man, a feeling that impelled him and

Sister Sackley to make the 140-mile journey from Aba to try to find him. When they arrived at the university, President Sackley was able to verify quickly that there was indeed a Professor Ikeme in the Department of Food Science. Unfortunately, he was told, the man was on vacation and was not on campus that day. As he stood in the office, trying to find someone who knew where Dr. Ikeme could be located, a man there spoke up: "I know Dr. Ikeme. He lives very close to my home. He is at his home today. Follow me and I'll take you to him."

The Sackleys drove up to Dr. Ikeme's house and knocked at the door. It was opened by a man who glanced first at the car with the Church logo on the side and then at President Sackley. When President Sackley said, "I'm looking for Dr. Ikeme," the man replied with a smile, "I am Dr. Ikeme and you are the mission president. Welcome. I have been waiting six years for you." He then introduced his wife and three small children to President and Sister Sackley. Delighted to have found his man, President Sackley said, "Dr. Ikeme, are you a member of the Church?" In response the professor took him to a back room where clothes hung on an indoor clothesline. Now all was clear to President Sackley. "Dr. Ikeme, I see that you are an endowed member of the Church." Brother Ikeme replied, "A very committed endowed member of the Church." One of the elect of God had been found.

For six years Ike Ikeme had faithfully lived in obedience to all of the covenants he had made in the holy temple, not knowing if he would ever again have the opportunity to fellowship with the Saints in mortality. During that time he maintained contact with the missionaries who had taught him in America. One of them, a woman in Salt Lake City, Utah, wrote to him regularly, advising him that he should never lose faith, for the day would come when he could reestablish contact with the Church. Thus sustained, Ike worked and prayed and endured. He told his wife, "I have waited in the Lord's time. You know the Lord's time is the best time."

Ike is married to a beautiful young woman named Patience, who has a master's degree in nutrition from the University of Nigeria and has been offered a prestigious scholarship to complete her doctorate at Cambridge University in England. Though Patience was not a member of the Church at the time President Sackley found her husband, her virtue and love of God shone in her face.

Before she met Ike, Patience was determined not to marry for some years, and certainly not to marry anyone from her home area, because of the type of men in that community. Ike was persistent, however, and she finally agreed to go out with him once, but only once. On that occasion she pointed out that she was a committed Christian. What, she asked, was Ike's religious affiliation, if any? He replied, "I am a Mormon." Patience was puzzled. She knew nothing about Mormons. "What is a Mormon," she asked, "and what do they believe, and how do they act?" Ike told her, "You just watch me."

On hearing this story, the Sackleys asked Patience, "Well, after six years of marriage and three children, what have you learned by watching your husband?" Her reply: "I have learned the Church is true. It is true because my man is true. Nothing that he would be involved with could ever be untrue, and no other religion on earth could cause him to live the wonderful life he lives in our home." What a wonderful example of love and devotion that statement portrays! How great is the power of example!

Ike Ikeme, noble and righteous priesthood bearer that he is, told President Sackley, "I want Patience to be taught the gospel without any pressure from me. I want her to accept the gospel for herself and not because of any influence I might exert." One day soon thereafter the Sackleys drove again to the university, looking for directions to Ike's home. They found Patience, who waved frantically to them. "Why have you come?" she asked. "To teach you the gospel," President Sackley replied.

95

"That is what I want," said Patience. "Can you come to our home and start right now?"

On November 19, 1987, Patience Ikeme was baptized by her husband, Ike, and confirmed a member of the Church by President Sackley. Just six months later Ike Ikeme was called to preside over the Enugu District of the Nigeria Aba Mission. A dynamic, energetic, loving leader, he will do great things for the Lord in Nigeria.

The First Black Members in Nigeria

Anthony Uzodimma Obinna and his wife, Fidelia Njoku Obinna, were the first black members of the Church in Nigeria. His second given name, Uzodimma, is his African name, given to him by his parents; it means "the best way" or "where the way is good or gainful, no one recognizes the leader, but where it is bad and has no gains, the leader is condemned and receives all the blame." In the Igbo tongue, Obinna means "one who is dear to his father."

Anthony, the fifth child of his parents, was born in 1928 in the village of Aboh Mbaise, Imo State, in eastern Nigeria. His father, Ugochukwu ("gift of God") Obinna, was a farmer, trader, and local judge, as well as an idol worshipper and polygamist. Each year Anthony's parents promised their gods gifts of goats, sheep. and chickens, as well as fruits and vegetables, to protect their lives and those of their families. Ugochukwu was a peacemaker, a lover of truth who hated falsehoods and evil, and was influential in his community.

It was not easy to get an education when Anthony was a boy. At that time Nigerians were afraid of white men and wanted nothing to do with them. They disliked anyone who wanted their children to go to school, preferring instead that their children remain at home to engage in subsistence agriculture. Only children who were considered as unhelpful members of the family were allowed to go to school.

In 1937 an English visitor spoke to Anthony's father; frustrated because he couldn't understand the foreigner, Ugo-chukwu decided Anthony should go to school. Off the youth went, first to local schools and later to schools in Jos, a town in northern Nigeria.

Anthony started teaching school in 1952. Two years before, he had married Fidelia, an orphan who supported younger brothers and sisters by working as a petty trader. Though she had no opportunity to receive an education, she was honest, diligent, and an outstanding example to other women. She patiently worked and struggled while Anthony finished four years of teacher training. But God had a work for Anthony Obinna that was greater than that as a teacher. He tells the story in his own words:

> In November 1965, I was visited in a dream by a tall person carrying a walking stick in his right hand. He asked whether I had read about Christian and Christiana from *A Pilgrim's Progress* by John Bunyan. I told him that I had forgotten it, and he told me to read it again. After a few months the same personage appeared to me again and took me to a most beautiful building and showed me everything in it. That personage appeared to me three times.
>
> During the Nigerian civil war, when we were confined to the house, I picked up an old copy of the *Reader's Digest* for September 1958. I opened it at page 34 and saw a picture of the same beautiful building I had been shown around in my dream, and immediately I recognized it. The heading was "The March of the Mormons." I had never before heard the word *Mormons*. I started to read the story because of the picture of the building I had seen in my dream. I discovered that it was all about The Church of Jesus Christ of Latter-day Saints.
>
> From the time I finished reading the story, I had no rest of mind any longer. My whole attention was focused on my new discovery. I rushed out immediately to tell my brothers, who were all amazed and

97

Anthony and Fedelia Obinna, first black member of the Church in Nigeria, with Elder Alexander B. Morrison

astonished to hear the story. ("Voice from Nigeria," *Ensign,* December 1980, p. 30.)

Because of the civil war, Anthony was unable to write to Church headquarters for more information at that time. When the blockade ended in 1971, he was able to get a letter through, and in response he received pamphlets, tracts, and a copy of the Book of Mormon. Though he was told the Church could not at that time be organized in Nigeria, Anthony continued to read and pray, asking God to open the door for him and his family.

He soon encountered persecutions, name calling, and abuse, but was conditioned by his conviction: "I knew I had discovered the truth, and men's threats could not move me and my group."

Finally the great day came. On November 21, 1978, a few months after the revelation on the priesthood, nineteen persons in Nigeria were baptized by Elders Rendell N. Mabey, Edwin Q. Cannon, Jr., and A. Bruce Knudsen. Among them were Anthony and Fidelia Obinna. The Aboh Mbaise Branch was organized, with Anthony Obinna as president, his brothers

Francis and Raymond as his counselors, and Fidelia as Relief Society president. The new branch presidency promptly reported the event in an ecstatic letter to the First Presidency:

> Dear Brethren,
>
> The entire members of The Church of Jesus Christ of Latter-day Saints in this part of Nigeria have the pleasure to thank you and the Latter-day Saints throughout the world for opening the door for the Gospel to come to our people in its fullness.
>
> We are happy for the many hours in the Upper Room of the Temple you spent supplicating the Lord to bring us into the fold. We thank our Heavenly Father for hearing your prayers and ours and by revelation has confirmed the long promised day, and has granted the holy priesthood to us, with the power to exercise its divine authority and enjoy every blessings of the temple. . . .
>
> There is no doubt that the Church here will grow and become a mighty centre for the Saints and bring progress enough to the people of Nigeria as it is doing all over the world.

I first met Anthony Obinna in 1983, while visiting eastern Nigeria in connection with a Thrasher Research Fund project. Two things stand out in my memory of the visit, and both illustrate the quality of the man. First, I was touched to note the love and respect he showed to his old "aunties" (his father's polygamous wives) and other members of his extended family. Second, as we sat in his comfortable but humble home he asked, "And how is the prophet?" My eyes filled with tears as I realized that he, who had never seen the prophet (President Kimball) and probably never would in mortality, still revered and respected him. I was touched by Anthony's humble goodness and deep spiritual nature.

Anthony and Fidelia are the parents of seven children, all active members of the Church. A man of great dignity and stature, he is a trustee of the Church in Nigeria. His brothers Francis and Raymond serve, respectively, as counselor to the president of the Nigeria Aba Mission and as counselor to the president of the Owerri Nigeria District. By their faithfulness and continued devotion, Anthony and Fidelia demonstrate they have not lost the vision obtained two decades ago. Recently they were privileged to be sealed for time and all eternity in the Logan Temple in Utah—the culmination of a long-held dream.

Other Faithful Saints

Not all Africans who join the Church do so in Africa. Many African students go to the United Kingdom, the United States, or elsewhere for schooling and not uncommonly encounter the Church in that foreign setting. Ronke Adefioye, a nineteen-year-old Nigerian woman from Ibadan, for example, went to the United Kingdom in 1987 to complete her university entrance studies. Raised a Muslim in Ibadan, she accepted the gospel and joined the Church after just two months in England. As well as successfully completing her studies, she has been an outstanding stake missionary and assistant nursery leader in the Peckham Ward of the Wandsworth England Stake. She plans to obtain a degree in accountancy at Brigham Young University and then return to her native Nigeria, where she will work and will help build up the Church, especially by teaching her family the truth of the restored gospel.

The story of Jill and John Ehanire begins in the mid-1960s, in the little market town of Alton, Hampshire, England. It was there that Jill first met John in Alton General Hospital. She was a nursing student and he, a young Nigerian physician, was undertaking postgraduate studies in England. Despite their racial and cultural differences, they fell in love and soon married. They had been married about two years and had two small sons when the missionaries first came to their home in April 1968. At that time they lived in Pontypool in north Wales, where John worked as a physician in the local hospital while awaiting a more permanent position in London. The mission-

John Ehanire,
who joined the Church
in England, and Elder
Alexander B. Morrison

aries gave Jill a copy of the Book of Mormon and she experienced a distinct feeling it was true, but because the family was in the process of moving, the missionaries' visit was soon forgotten.

The missionaries recontacted Jill a few weeks after the family arrived in London. Jill began to investigate the Church, was deeply impressed by what she found, and was soon baptized, on November 29, 1968. But her conversion was not without struggle and pain. Although she had a testimony that the gospel is true, she was devastated to learn that John, whom she dearly loved, could not receive the priesthood. Upset and confused, she poured out her heart to her Father in heaven. Why, she asked, had she gained a testimony of the Savior and His church, only to find that her beloved husband was denied God's priesthood?

As she knelt in prayer, a feeling of deep calm gradually came over her. "It was as if a voice said to me very firmly but gently, 'Don't worry, have faith,' " she recalled. "It was as if a great load had been lifted from my shoulders and I was immediately free from the distress I had felt earlier. Greatly comforted and assured, I went to bed early and slept very soundly. The next day I experienced the same wonderful feeling of calm, faith, and courage, replacing doubt and fear."

After her baptism, Jill struggled to stay active in the Church. Often she was encouraged back to church only through the loving kindness of visiting teachers and missionaries. Through it all, John was loving and supportive of her. He studied with the missionaries, challenging them repeatedly with probing questions. Though he was twice their age, he recognized that those young men spoke the words of truth, as God's legal representatives. Though the priesthood barrier was a major test of his faith, John was baptized on October 3, 1970, in the Romford chapel near London.

Sadly, doubts inspired by the priesthood issue crept into John's mind and prevented his active participation in the program of the Church for some time. Jill too continued to struggle with her faith. To compound the problem, the family moved in 1972 back to Nigeria, where John had been offered a good position in a new teaching hospital in his home town of Benin City. The Ehanires had no contact with the Church, save for an occasional letter from friends, for several years.

In 1978, while glancing through a local Nigerian newspaper, Jill saw a photograph showing a black couple from Utah, with the explanation that worthy black men now could receive the priesthood in The Church of Jesus Christ of Latter-day Saints. Immediately the realization of that divine assurance she had received more than ten years before flooded into her mind. "A joy came to me which no words can describe," she said, "and I hurried to give John the good news."

Four years later, in 1982, a branch of the Church was organized in Benin City. The missionaries soon found the Ehanires, who welcomed them with open arms. Jill recalls, "After they left that evening I cried with happiness and thanked the

Lord for sending His church to Nigeria and for allowing John and me back into the fold again."

Dr. John Ehanire, chief medical officer at the University of Benin, currently serves as president of the Benin District of the Church. He is a good physician and, much more importantly, a good man, one who loves his family and honors the priesthood of God he bears. A warm and gentle man, he is the soul of kindness. I am honored to call him my friend.

CHAPTER SEVEN

Ghana's Golden Harvest

Ghana, the "Black Star of Africa," is a country roughly the size of England, Scotland, and Wales. Shaped somewhat like a box, it lies near the equator on the Gulf of Guinea and consequently is very hot and steamy. Tropical rain forest starts almost at the ocean's edge and gives way to heavily forested hills in the north, but much of the center of the country is made up of scrub-covered plains, traversed by the White and Black Volta rivers and numerous other streams. Lake Volta stretches for many miles north and south in the eastern part of the country. Approximately half of Ghana is less than 500 feet above sea level.

When it was a British colony, Ghana was known as the Gold Coast. Although some gold has indeed been produced in the country since time immemorial, the term "Gold Coast" originated from a description of the money that changed hands in an evil and monstrous business, one that epitomizes man's inhumanity to man—the slave trade. No one knows for certain how many Africans, including Ghanaians, were sold into slavery, but estimates range as high as fifty million. Probably a more accurate estimate would be ten to fifteen million from West Africa, with another five to ten million from East Africa. The slave trade between West Africa and the Americas peaked in the late eighteenth century, with 700,000 persons being transported under hideously inhumane conditions in the last decade of the century alone. Most were young adults aged fifteen to thirty-five, selected like beasts of burden for their ability to bear children or do brutally hard manual labor in the cotton fields and sugar plantations of the New World. Before transportation, they were held like caged animals in pens while Arab traders bargained for their price with European and American ship owners. One in seven died during the long sea voyage.

Africans themselves, as well as the Arab traders and white shippers, were guilty of operating the slave trade. All must bear a portion of the shame and guilt. Many slaves were prisoners captured in one tribal war or another and sold by their African captors. Others were debtors, outcasts, or those who by misadventure had wandered across the boundaries of another tribe's territory and were captured by a tribal chief prepared to traffic in human flesh for profit. The slave trade enriched kings in the interior of Ghana and other African countries and feathered the pockets of African merchants and middlemen on the coast.

A major factor that led to the end of the slave trade was the decision by the British government in 1807 to bar its citizens from slave trading. The Royal Navy established an antislavery patrol of twenty ships, which detained nearly 1,300 slave ships and freed 130,000 slaves in the period from 1825 to 1865. During that time, however, well over a million slaves were slipped through the blockade and taken to the Americas. Not until the American Civil War was over did trafficking in slaves end in the United States.

Ghana became Black Africa's first ex-colony when it achieved independence from Britain in 1957. Albeit somewhat belatedly, the British had recognized the inevitability of independence and had tried to prepare the country for that day. Whites were not allowed to settle in Ghana and had to receive government approval before they could even seek employment. There were only a few thousand colonial administrators, and a state council largely ran local affairs. Furthermore the country was, and still is, rich in natural resources, including manganese (it was the world's major exporter in 1957), bauxite, diamonds, and gold. Ghana produces and exports vast quantities of cocoa and is one of the major cocoa producers in the world. Of greatest importance, its people are intelligent, clever, and ingenious, with a reputation for resiliency, for never losing their heads, and for staying cool even under the most adverse conditions.

Why, then, is Ghana not better off today than it is? Why are the slums of Accra and Takoradi so depressing and squalid? Why is there so much poverty? At least part of the answer lies in the plunder and pillage carried out by many of Ghana's leaders over the past thirty years. One after another they systematically looted the country of its riches, until the Black Star of Africa became a nation of beggars living in abject poverty. Thankfully, the current leader, Flight Lieutenant Jerry Rawlings, is trying very hard to undo many of the errors of the past. As a young thirty-two-year-old Ghanaian officer, he removed a dictator, General Akuffo, from power in a coup in 1979, then handed the reins of government over to a civilian regime. The new regime's indolence and corruption so disgusted him that he overthrew it on New Year's Eve in 1981. Since then, over 80,000 civil servants have been dismissed, and Ghanaians have begun to face up to the hard truths of economics. The Ghanaian unit of currency, the cedi, has been devalued and import prices have shot up. Most importantly, however, since 1983 the gross domestic product has increased by an average of 6 percent per year, and the government gets full marks from the World Bank and the International Monetary Fund for at least beginning the long, hard turnaround needed if the country is ever to achieve its potential.

Mention has been made of the ingenuity of the Ghanaian people. I thought of that a few months ago as I drove along the coastal road between Accra and Cape Coast with our then mission president, Miles Cunningham. As we drove along what would have been a million-dollar-a-mile beach in California,

Fishermen pull net
full of fish ashore
on African beach

we watched a group of fishermen at work. One end of a large net was attached to a rope secured to a sturdy palm tree along the shore, and the net itself was towed by a small boat out into the ocean about four hundred yards or more, until it formed a great half circle. The free end of the net, attached to a rope, was then slowly tugged toward shore by a dozen or more men. The process of bringing the net ashore would take several hours, and if the fishermen were lucky they would land a catch of hundreds of pounds of fish. Technically, this form of fishing is called seine-net fishing. I was impressed by this simple yet ingenious use of resources.

In the spirit of adventure, and perhaps because each of us still retains a large streak of small boy inside him, President Cunningham and I stopped to give them a hand. For several minutes we tugged and hauled on the rope in response to the chanted cadence of the chief among the fishermen. The men laughed and joked, too courteous to comment on our somewhat puny efforts, and when we left they thanked us profusely. It was an elemental, almost primeval, scene, not much changed, I suppose, from what it would have been hundreds of years ago, an experience that lives in my memory as an example of the unchangeable face of Africa.

I felt a kinship to those simple fishermen, though we only exchanged smiles and a few words, and I remembered how the Savior had labored among men like that—men who knew the roar of the waves and the smell of the sea—and how He called some of them to be "fishers of men." I thought of Peter, the apostle, himself a fisherman, whose hands undoubtedly were rough and calloused and whose face was as weather-beaten and wind-burned as the faces of my Ghanaian brothers, and of how he would have felt at home among them.

As I witnessed their poverty and need, my thoughts turned to the great story told with majestic power and passion in John 21. Peter and others of the apostles had fished all night without success. When morning came they saw a man standing on the shore. He called to them to cast their net on the right side of the ship. They did so and were rewarded with a catch so numerous they could not draw it in. Later, Jesus (for He it was who had called to them) fed them fish and bread and spoke these immortal words to Peter: "Feed my lambs; feed my sheep." *Oh,* I thought, *how great is our responsibility to feed you, my African brothers—to feed you with that spiritual food which will bring you eternal life, the glorious gospel of the living Christ!* I was heartened by the human contact, sobered by the realization of the magnitude of the task that lies ahead for the Church in Africa, and more aware than ever that He who called Peter has also called latter-day servants to be "fishers of men."

The Church Comes to Ghana

The Church came to Ghana in 1979 with the creation of the West African Mission. As in Nigeria, the first missionaries found numerous small congregations of truth seekers who had started their own religious organizations, patterned after The Church of Jesus Christ of Latter-day Saints, right down to the name. The knowledge on which these groups were based was fragmentary and sometimes distorted. It had been accumulated over the years by Ghanaians who had studied in the United States or the United Kingdom or who had received missionary tracts in response to their requests to Church headquarters. Within the limits of their understanding, however, they did their best to set up and follow Church procedures and practices. Of course, they lacked priesthood authority for what they were doing, and they had to be taught and baptized in the Lord's way. So prepared were the people of Ghana to receive the gospel message, however, that growth of that portion of the West African Mission was rapid.

By the time the Ghana Accra Mission was established in July 1985, there were some 3,000 members in Ghana. Even before then, however, the first Ghanaian missionaries had been called. Elder Benjamin Crosby Sampson-Davis and Elder Samuel E. Bainson were called in early 1981 to serve in the England Manchester Mission. Before he heard of the Church, Elder Sampson-Davis had planned to enter the Anglican ministry, but when the Spirit touched his heart, he gladly gave it all up, turning down a four-year scholarship to an Anglican theological school in Nigeria. His companion, Elder Bainson, was a great missionary even prior to his call, having been responsible for the baptism of several friends. He prayed to be found worthy to serve a mission for the Lord, and his prayers were answered. "Because I've accepted the gospel, so many blessings have come to me," he says. "Sharing the gospel with somebody that doesn't have it is a special thing." (*Ensign,* April 1981, p. 78.)

In Ghana as elsewhere, missionaries submit a weekly report to their mission president. What a thrill it is to read those reports, which reveal the great faith and sweet spirit of the Ghanaian Saints. A recent report submitted by two Ghanaian missionaries, Sisters Essel and Mantey, indicates how in Ghana "the field is white already to harvest; and lo [she] that thrusteth in [her] sickle with [her] might, the same layeth up in store that [she] perisheth not, but bringeth salvation to [her] soul." (D&C 4:4.) In a single week they had fifty-one discussions, forty-nine of which resulted in a return appointment or baptism. Their weekly letter to the mission president reported: "One of the ways we've gained our sure knowledge that Jesus is the Christ and God is our Heavenly Father is through this our missionary service. We now understand that our Heavenly Father is gathering His family for a wonderful reunion, and we are helping. We had five souls for our baptism, which took place on Saturday 16/4/88 [April 16, 1988]. We were very happy for this mercy that our Heavenly Father showed us. This enabled us to believe that God is the rewarder of all those who diligently seek Him. We know the Church is true and everything in relation to it is also true. We say this in the name of our Lord and Saviour, Jesus Christ. Amen."

The faith and conviction of these choice young missionaries will result in a great harvest of souls in Ghana, as the elect of God hear the voices of His ordained servants. What is more, from the ranks of returned missionaries will come the bishops, stake presidents, and sister leaders of tomorrow.

Strong Leaders for the Church

As elsewhere in Black Africa, the Church in Ghana has attracted many outstanding men and women to its banners. One such stalwart is Professor Banyon A. Dadson, pro-vice chancellor (vice president) of the University of Cape Coast. A big man physically, intellectually, and spiritually, he holds a Ph.D. in organic chemistry from one of the world's great universities, Cambridge University in England. Prior to his current appointment, he served as professor of chemistry and then dean of faculty at his university. His professional credentials are more than matched by his spiritual strength. The story of his conversion is an interesting one. His first contact with Mormon teachings occurred in the early 1970s, when he met "Reverend" Billy Johnson, a Ghanaian who had come across a copy of the Book of Mormon and had started his own religious organization based on its teachings, but without official authority from The Church of Jesus Christ of Latter-day Saints. Brother Dadson attended one of the meetings of the group, but he had difficulty accepting the dancing and drumming that were part of the service. He was searching for the true gospel of Christ but felt that Johnson's organization fell short of the mark.

Nearly a decade later, Billy Johnson again contacted Brother Dadson. This time he told him that The Church of Jesus Christ of Latter-day Saints had come officially to Ghana, that a branch had been organized with priesthood authority, and that he, Billy Johnson, had been baptized and called as the first district president.

Brother Dadson came back to church. He soon realized that he had finally found the pearl of great price for which he had been seeking. He was baptized, as were his wife, Henrietta, and the four oldest of their six children. As so often happens, his professional career has been furthered by his Church membership. "The Church has made me a more effective teacher and leader," he explains. "In dealing with the staff, I am constrained by the law of Christ to show love." (*Ensign,* June 1986, p. 58.)

Emmanuel Abu Kissi, a physician and surgeon, is another Ghanaian who combines great spiritual strength with unusual talents and abilities. He and his wife, Benedicta Lizabeth, first heard of the Church in England in the late 1970s. At the time, Brother Kissi was completing a three-year residency in surgery, and the family lived in Macclesfield, just outside of Manchester. Sister Kissi, a trained nurse/midwife, was in the midst of a spiritual depression so severe she had quit work and, in constant fear she would die, remained at home in their apartment.

111

Emmanuel Abu Kissi, a physician in Ghana, was converted to the Church in England

One day she called Emmanuel, excited and bubbling with enthusiasm, to announce that she was going back to work. Her husband was, of course, delighted but surprised. What, he asked, had happened to change her attitude? She explained that missionaries from The Church of Jesus Christ of Latter-day Saints had come to her door. They talked for a few minutes, and, sensing they could help her, she asked for a priesthood blessing. Instantly the feeling of spiritual depression that had haunted and tortured her for many weeks left, not to return.

The Kissis were taught by the missionaries, but Brother Kissi had questions about the Church no one seemed able to satisfy. Anxious to receive an answer, he sat down to write President Spencer W. Kimball. He recalls: "Just before I put pen to paper, all the answers I wanted became clear. To this day I can't remember the questions."

Brother Kissi has deep compassion for the poor. He and his family could have stayed in Great Britain after the completion of his surgical training and would have enjoyed a much higher standard of living than in Ghana. Yet he was anxious to return home. "The British people *wanted* me, but my people *needed* me," he explains.

Emmanuel and Benedicta operate a small hospital in Accra, appropriately named Deseret Hospital. Though ill equipped by Western standards, it is clean and neat and provides facilities desperately needed by the people of Ghana. Brother Kissi's generous, loving heart and deep compassion for those who suffer will not let him turn anyone away, regardless of ability to pay. During a 1983 drought in Ghana he helped distribute rice, corn, and beans sent by the Church to aid members and nonmembers alike. The gratitude of those who were helped by the gift of life-saving food touched his heart and often brought tears to his eyes. Emmanuel Kissi will probably never be rich in the things of this world, but he has learned well the lesson so eloquently summarized by King Benjamin: "When ye are in the service of your fellow beings ye are only in the service of your God." (Mosiah 2:17.) He exemplifies not only the highest ideals of the medical profession, but also those of Christian charity, which "endureth forever; and whoso is found possessed of it at the last day, it shall be well with him." (Moroni 7:47.) Brother Kissi's story, which I have heard from his own lips on several occasions, was told in *Church News,* November 23, 1986.

In Ghana, as elsewhere in Black Africa, sharing and mutual help in times of need are deeply held social values. President Emmanuel Opare, second counselor in the Accra District presidency. tells this faith-promoting story: He was home one weekend with his wife and four small children. Like most African families, the Opares are poor; all the money they had to see them through the weekend was eighty cedis, then equivalent to about one dollar. A man came to the door saying that he needed to go home and had no money for transportation. President Opare felt impressed to give him fifty cedis, even though that almost totally depleted the family's meager resources. Later that day an old school friend came by to visit. The two men had not seen each other for several years and enjoyed visiting together for most of the evening, reminiscing about old times and mutual friends. For a few hours, at least, Emmanuel was able to forget his financial problems. Later that evening, as the friend left, he gave President Opare a present of 5,000 cedis (sixty dollars).

Elizabeth Kwaw, a district Relief Society president and seminary teacher in Cape Coast, exemplifies the great faith of the women of Ghana. During the 1983–84 famine in Ghana she was approached by one of her neighbors, who said, "How is it that we are getting slim but you and your husband continue to be strong and robust?" As Sister Kwaw tells this story, she testifies that the principle of tithing kept her and her family going during that terrible time. Each night she would lie in bed and pray fervently that Heavenly Father would bless her to know what to make or sell in her small store in order to bring in the cash necessary to buy food for her family. She was inspired to sell hush puppies, fried pastries made of cornmeal and spices, and got up at three o'clock in the morning to make several hundred of these tasty snacks daily. She had learned to make them in the United States. Although hush puppies are not a usual part of the Ghanaian diet, sales were brisk, and the proceeds kept her family going. She was careful to pay tithing on her income and grateful to be able to do so, though it would have been so easy, under the circumstances, to forget about the Lord's tenth. Sister Kwaw laughs when she thinks about making and selling such a foreign food, but she is convinced that the Lord inspired her to do so.

Sister Kwaw's husband, Stephen, shakes his head in amazement as he tells about the customers and business in Elizabeth's small store. In a land where everyone has to work at whatever they can find in order to barely scratch out a living, Sister Kwaw's store is very important to the family, even though her husband, Stephen, has a good job, by Ghanaian standards at least.

While serving as district Relief Society president, Elizabeth, assisted by her counselors, cooked lunches for missionary zone conferences every six weeks, as well as for other district functions and activities. Because of these church-service activities, she found it necessary to close her store several days each month during busy selling times. To the amazement of others, business lost from closing the store was always made up the day before or in the days immediately following the closure. Her husband laughs when he recounts that customers would even come to their home outside of regular store hours asking to buy a dress, though dresses of comparable quality could be purchased readily at numerous retail outlets all over town. Elizabeth and Stephen know from experience that when we are on the Lord's errand, He blesses us. They testify to the sweet fulfillment in their lives of the Savior's words: "Give and it shall be given unto you; good measure, pressed down, and shaken together, and running over, shall men give into your bosom. For with the same measure that ye mete withal it shall be measured to you again." (Luke 6:38.)

Tracey Addy is a vivacious sixteen-year-old Ghanaian who lives in the city of Tema, just east of Accra, with her parents, Isaac and June, and her four brothers and a sister. The Addys, who are a strong Latter-day Saint family, moved back to Ghana from England a few years ago. Though the adjustments in living style and standards have sometimes been challenging, Tracey and her brothers and sister have been assisted greatly by the examples of their parents.

At a recent district conference in Accra, Tracey spoke of her membership in the Church and how its standards help her to withstand temptation. Said she: "I am glad to be a member of this church, because it makes me different from others, especially in school. My moral standards are different from theirs, [which include,] for example, going out late, never staying at home, wearing dresses or clothes that give bad ideas, and having close relationships with boys. I like to have the moral courage to make my actions consistent with my knowledge of right and wrong. This also helps me to keep far away from trouble.

"Two good examples of strong leaders in this church are my mum and dad. I know my dad works very hard for this church and is devoted to serving it. He gets up early in the morning and comes home to carry on with more work at his desk late at night. And also my mum, who helps the Relief Society and does a lot of work at the district meetings.

"I hope that one day I'll grow up to be like them. I know that Satan works very hard to pull us down, but we can overcome him by prayer and fasting. He can try to tempt us through friends. But if we hold on tight to the iron rod, he'll never be able to catch us. And if we sow the righteous seed in our lives, we will one day be rewarded for our efforts."

How impressed I was with this sweet young woman, with her calm determination to live the standards of the Church and her earnest desire to serve the Lord. I recalled the ringing words of the First Presidency: "How glorious and near to the angels is youth that is clean. This youth has joy unspeakable here and eternal happiness hereafter."

Young Latter-day Saints in Ghana and elsewhere in Black Africa face the same problems as their counterparts in other countries of the world — conflicting priorities, getting and keeping a testimony, the temptations of the flesh, loneliness, career choices, and so forth. Because Latter-day Saints are very much a minority group in African society, some of those problems may seem accentuated, but though temptation may alter its disguise, the challenge is constant worldwide. It is, therefore, gratifying to listen to a dedicated young person such as Tracey, and to realize that she and many more like her represent the promise of tomorrow for the Church in Africa.

In June 1989, without any warning, the government of

Relief Society sisters in Nigerian branch

Ghana issued an injunction that suspended activities of The Church of Jesus Christ of Latter-day Saints and another church in the country. All expatriate missionaries were required to leave Ghana within seven days, our buildings were locked, and no meetings were permitted. The devil and his agents rejoiced.

After some difficulty, acting under instructions from the First Presidency and the Council of the Twelve Apostles, Elder Jack H. Goaslind and I were able to visit Ghana and discuss the matter with senior officials of the government. It was obvious to us they had been misled by professional revilers of the Church into believing scurrilous lies about the Latter-day Saints and their beliefs. The officials were unaware of the revelation on priesthood and of the Church's teachings on the brotherhood of man. They also seemed not to know of the very substantial amounts of humanitarian aid provided by the Church over the years to the people of Ghana, assistance provided in the true spirit of brotherhood and Christian charity.

As always, our faithful members in Ghana have obediently

117

followed the requirement that we honor, obey, and sustain the law of the land, and they have humbly accepted the government's decision. But the flame of faith continues to burn strong and true in their hearts as they anxiously await the day when the injunction will be lifted and they can once again meet to worship God in purity and power. We have the assurance of the Spirit that that day will come soon.

Ghana's golden harvest of souls, which started as a trickle only a decade ago, will in God's time grow steadily into a great torrent. It will roll forward "till, like a sea of glory, it spreads from pole to pole" (*Hymns,* 1985, no. 268), across the length and breadth of that ancient land, and the Black Star of Africa sparkles with the effulgent beauty of the glorious gospel of Christ.

CHAPTER EIGHT

Brave Beginnings in Other Countries

In addition to our major thrusts into Nigeria and Ghana, brave beginnings have been made to bring the restored gospel of Christ to the inhabitants of a number of other countries in Black Africa. Much, of course, needs to be done everywhere. We are just beginning to get our feet firmly under us in those countries. Yet "mighty oaks from small acorns grow," and we can have confidence that the Church will go forward in these and all other lands in Africa, on the Lord's timetable, to bring the peace and joy of the everlasting gospel to all of God's children in that great continent.

Here are brief summaries of the current state of the growth of the Church in various countries of Africa.

Ivory Coast

The Ivory Coast, a West African country known also by its French name as Cote d'Ivoire, has a population of approximately ten million, of whom two million or so live in Abidjan, the capital. Other large towns include Bouake, Yamoussoukro, and Daloa. Abidjan, which has many modern buildings and shops, has been called "the Paris of Africa." Certainly the French influence remains strong there. Although France formally severed ties with her former colony more than twenty-five years ago, French advisers, money, and influence are felt everywhere.

Members of The Church of Jesus Christ of Latter-day Saints have lived and worked in Ivory Coast over the past twenty or more years. For most of this time they operated under the auspices of the former International Mission, which attempted to maintain contact with scattered expatriate families in the country. During the 1970s, Barnard Silver and his wife, Cherry, for example, lived in Ferkessedougou, 300 miles up-country from Abidjan, where he was the general manager of a large sugar mill. During this time the Silvers conducted sacrament and Sunday School meetings in their home and visited scattered members throughout the country as they were able to do so. Similarly, Terry Don Broadhead and his wife, Bobby, held meetings in their home in 1986 and 1987. Brother Broadhead is a U.S. military man temporarily assigned to Ivory Coast.

As mentioned in chapter 5, Elder Marvin J. Ashton dedicated the land of Ivory Coast for the preaching of the gospel on September 4, 1987, and set Brother Broadhead apart to serve as the unit leader, with authority to baptize, ordain, and set in order the affairs of the Church in Abidjan. Brother Broadhead now has been released, and Philippe Assard, a native Ivorian, serves as branch president in Abidjan.

Documentation to have the Church officially recognized by the Ivory Coast government was submitted in the spring of 1987. The application still awaited approval as of spring 1990, when this was written, but hopes were high this could be accomplished soon. In the meantime, two faithful expatriate missionary couples, Scott H. and Lu Ciel Taggart[1] and Robert M. and Lola Mae Walker, were busily engaged in bringing souls to Christ in Ivory Coast, laboring in Abidjan, where more than 100 individuals have joined the Church since early 1988.

---

[1]Elder Taggart has subsequently been called to serve as mission president in Zaire. He and Sister Taggart took up their duties in July 1990.

As is common in Black Africa, many of the Saints in Ivory Coast experience extreme financial stress. Many heads of families have no work. The unemployment rate approaches 80 percent. Though many of our members are well trained in various occupations and desperately want to work, they cannot find jobs. The Ivory Coast is extremely depressed economically, primarily as a result of the current low world prices for coffee and cocoa, the country's primary exports.

Despite their extreme temporal difficulties, however, the Saints in Ivory Coast evince the same spirit of faith and testimony so common among Latter-day Saints in Africa. They have found an age-old truth, one that has applied to Christians over the centuries: to follow the path of Christ requires faith, courage, and sacrifice. Lucien Affoue, his wife, Agathe, and their children, Patricia, Clarissa, and Geoffrey, for example, illustrate the courage and fortitude of the Ivorian Saints. Brother Affoue joined the Church in Lyon, France, in 1980, while a student. Although Patricia and Clarissa, the two daughters, also joined the Church, at first Agathe wanted nothing to do with her husband's new faith. One day, however, moved by the Spirit, she went to the missionaries and asked to be taught. Soon she too joined, and the family was later sealed for time and all eternity in the Swiss Temple.

While residing in France, Brother and Sister Affoue gained valuable church experience, he in the presidency of the Bordeaux Branch and she as a counselor in Primary. In March 1984 the family returned to Ivory Coast, where Brother Affoue hoped to obtain a teaching position. For two years they were the only Saints in the country. Each week Brother Affoue faithfully held church services for his family in their home. Finally, in 1986, the Affoues received a letter from Philippe Assard, who with his family had returned to his native country from Germany. Brother Assard had joined the Church in Germany and served in the high council of the Dusseldorf Germany Stake. Sister Assard, who is a native German, struggled to learn

French and adapt to her new surroundings in Africa. Despite their cultural differences, she and Sister Affoue became fast friends, bound together by the sisterhood of the gospel. Each week the Affoue and Assard families met for church services at the home of the Assards and rejoiced together as they shared their testimonies of the truthfulness of the great latter-day work.

A highlight of these first stirrings of church growth in Ivory Coast was the visit in early 1987 of Elder Russell M. Taylor, then of the Europe Area presidency. Elder Taylor blessed and encouraged the members and authorized Brother Assard to gather together members of the Church and to serve as "shepherd of the flock" in Ivory Coast. How the Affoue family rejoiced as growth began to occur!

In October 1987 Brother Affoue was finally able to obtain employment, as professor of automotive science in a technical college at Bouake, the second largest city in Ivory Coast. Once again the family moved, and once again they were the only members of the Church in their part of the country. Faithful as ever, they held sacrament meeting and Sunday School in their home. A unit of the Church has now been organized in Bouake, with more than twenty members attending each week. Brother Affoue serves as unit leader, with Sister Affoue looking after Relief Society and Young Women, and Clarissa teaching Primary.

The Affoue children are as faithful as their parents. When Patricia came home for Christmas in 1987, she began to teach the Primary lessons to her younger brother and other children. After she left, Clarissa, age thirteen, said to her father, "Now give *me* a chance to teach the children." Clarissa and a non-member cousin now work with a group that began with four children and has expanded to nearly a dozen.

Solange Sea, aged twenty-five, is the first Ivoirian woman to be baptized into the Church in Ivory Coast. The mother of two small children, Ezekiel and Sarah, she is married to Vincent Sea, a technician with the national electric energy company, and also a member of the Church. Solange, a tall, slender, intense woman, has deep spiritual sensitivities. I listened to the story of her conversion while attending a Church meeting in Abidjan in September 1988. When Solange and Vincent were introduced to missionaries Barnard and Cherry Silver in May 1988, she quickly began to read the Book of Mormon and various missionary tracts for several hours a day. She asked the missionaries whether the Angel Moroni looked like the picture in one of the tracts. Why? they asked. She replied, "One morning this week I had a vision of a heavenly being." At the heavenly visitor's request, she left the bedroom, brought back the two children, and awakened her husband to pray for them all. Vincent did not see the vision, but he understood the depth of his wife's conviction.

Not uncommon for Africans, Solange's testimony of the truthfulness of the gospel came in a dream. As she lay in bed, she saw Jesus approach her and tenderly ask, "Do you love me?" Overwhelmed by a sense of the Savior's love for her and her love for Him, Solange began to weep. She made a commitment to serve Him and accepted the invitation to be baptized. She was subsequently called to serve as a counselor in Relief Society. Her unusual spiritual sensitivity, great desire and commitment to serve, and generous spirit commend her to all.

Liberia

Liberia, with a land mass about the size of the state of Tennessee, is a small West African country that lies just north of the equator at a point where the coastline turns east. The history of Liberia is unlike that of any other African country. It owes its origin to freed black slaves who returned to the continent, their passage home to Africa paid for in the early 1800s by a white philanthropic society, the American Colonization Society, which was chartered by the U.S. Congress. Liberia's American origins are found everywhere in the country, from the name of its capital city, Monrovia (named after U.S. President James Monroe of Monroe Doctrine fame) to its red, white, and blue flag with a single star. The U.S. dollar is official currency, and many streets and townships bear American place-names.

For 133 years Liberia seemed to be a unique African example of rock-solid political stability. In 1971 it had the distinction of being the first African nation to achieve a peaceful constitutional transfer of power when President William Tubman died in office and was succeeded by his vice president, William Tolbert. Nine years later, in 1980, the government of President Tolbert was overthrown in a military coup led by a sergeant in the Liberian army named Samuel K. Doe, who promptly assumed the rank of general.

The Liberia Monrovia Mission was established in early 1988, with J. Duffy Palmer as mission president. Brother Palmer is a World War II veteran of the U.S. Marine Corps who was badly wounded in fighting in the Pacific. He returned from military service to study law and become a judge in Utah. Prior to their call to labor in Liberia, President Palmer and his wife, Jocelyn, served as missionaries in the Nigeria Lagos Mission, where President Palmer was mission president from 1984–1986. The Palmers thus were well suited to open up missionary work in another West African country. No more faithful or dedicated couple could have been found to undertake those crucial first steps involved in setting a new mission in place in Africa.

The Palmers arrived in Liberia several months before the Liberia Monrovia Mission was established and, with characteristic energy and enthusiasm, set to work. The first requirement was to establish the support systems so necessary for the survival of expatriates in Black Africa—safe housing of acceptable quality, an account with a reputable bank, an automobile, registration with appropriate government departments. Some may wonder about the designation of an automobile as a necessity, but our experience in Black Africa has shown that expatriate

124

missionaries simply cannot function there at present without one. Though driving conditions in Black African countries are an adventure at best, failure to have an automobile makes it well-nigh impossible for expatriates to shop for food and other essentials or visit investigators, and they are much safer in an automobile than they would be as pedestrians.

President and Sister Palmer were released from their missions in mid-1989 and returned to their Utah home. President Palmer was replaced by Miles Cunningham, a retired California businessman. President Cunningham and his vivacious wife, Stella, are "old African hands," having served previously in Ghana, where Brother Cunningham was mission president. Both possess in full measure those characteristics of resourcefulness, enthusiasm, and adaptability, coupled with deep spirituality, so essential for successful missionary work in Africa.

Liberia was dedicated for the preaching of the gospel in September 1987 by Elder Marvin J. Ashton of the Quorum of the Twelve. The apostolic blessing pronounced on the land and its people has resulted in steady growth of the Church in Liberia, and by the end of 1989 there were more than 1,000 members.

The great faith and simple reliance on the Lord of the Latter-day Saints in Liberia is illustrated in the following tender tale recounted recently by Sister Ruth F. Stewart, an American missionary in Monrovia:

"Two priesthood leaders, Brothers Jimmy Padmore and Franklin Kennedy, had come to a school where a small local congregation of the Saints meets, early one Saturday morning, to tidy up and prepare the sacrament table. As they poured the water into the cups, Brother Padmore looked at his friend anxiously and said he didn't have any money for the bread. Brother Kennedy sadly said he didn't have any either, and so they finished up in silence and neatly covered the small table with a snow-white cloth. As they locked the door, leaving the bread plate empty, Brother Padmore whispered, 'We'll have bread for the sacrament this morning.'

"As they began the long walk home to get their families, they approached a little stand where bread rolls were for sale. Brother Padmore looked down and saw a twenty-five cent piece lying in the sand. They purchased the rolls and, with big smiles and beaming faces, shook hands warmly and said, 'Brother, we have our sacrament.'"

As elsewhere in Black Africa, a key to real growth in Liberia is to allow—indeed, to insist—that Africans provide the leadership required. Expatriates can and should provide "shadow leadership" and training, but the faster Africans are encouraged to "govern themselves," in the words of the Prophet Joseph Smith, the faster the work will progress. President Cunningham fully understands that principle and is applying it with vigor and intelligence. Both extensive training and patience are required, but it is essential that the purity of the doctrine and practices of the Church be maintained.

The need is not so much to seek growth as to modulate it. It would readily be possible to baptize hundreds each week in Liberia, but the requirements for wisdom and orderliness indicate otherwise. Elder Ashton's wise words of counsel on this subject bear repetition. In remarks made shortly after returning from dedicating Liberia and two other African nations for the preaching of the gospel, he said that one of our challenges is to "not try to grow beyond our ability to prepare local leadership. Branches must not outgrow the roots." (*Church News,* October 17, 1987.) That is advice we must never forget as the Church forges forward in Liberia and other Black African countries.

Zaire

One of the most impressive things about the country of Zaire is its size. With fewer than 30 million people, it is three times the size of Texas and occupies much of central Africa.

126

Neighbors get together at village in Zaire

Zaire contains some of the world's densest rain forests, with giant trees towering overhead two hundred feet or more, forming a luminous green canopy that filters out direct sunlight. In the eastern part of the country are vast grassy savannas that, if properly cultivated, could provide huge amounts of the food so badly needed by the people of Zaire. (Of course, even if the food were grown, transporting it elsewhere in the country would pose a problem, since Zaire has at present less than four thousand miles of roads.)

Much of the northern border of the country is marked by the mighty Congo (Zaire) River, the second largest river by volume in the world. In their recurring and eventually successful attempts to find a sea route to the spices of the Orient, Portuguese sailors stopped at the mouth of the Congo in 1482. It was probably the first contact between Europeans and the Kongo Kingdom that flourished there. Until the last century, however, the major contact between the peoples of the Congo

127

and the West was through the hellish and inhuman trade in slaves. Thousands of frightened, brutalized people were transported from the region, many of them taken by Portuguese slave traders to work on Brazilian plantations.

By the late nineteenth century, the European powers were casting avaricious eyes on Africa, in search of cheap raw materials for their factories, new markets for manufactured goods, and better trade routes. King Leopold II of Belgium financed expeditions in the Congo region by H. M. Stanley, an explorer most famous for his part in finding the missionary-explorer David Livingstone, who had disappeared in central Africa. Stanley secured treaties with Congolese chiefs that permitted King Leopold to personally control a million square miles of central Africa. Leopold's Congo estate was later transferred to Belgium, and for many years the region was known as the Belgian Congo. Independence from Belgium was achieved in 1960, and the new rulers, wishing to shed their colonial past, renamed the country Zaire.

The official language of Zaire is French, spoken by most men but by only a minority of women, who, as in other Black African countries, are in general less educated than their male counterparts. More than two hundred local languages are spoken. At a recent sacrament meeting in Kinshasa, the capital, for example, I spoke in French, which the brethren present could understand, and was simultaneously translated into Linguala, a local tongue, for the benefit of the sisters. In the south of Zaire, a variation of Swahili (Shaba-swahili) is widely used. It differs somewhat from the Swahili spoken in eastern Africa.

When The Church of Jesus Christ of Latter-day Saints was granted legal status by the government of Zaire on February 12, 1986, there were only a few members of the Church in that vast country. David M. Kennedy, special representative of the First Presidency, met on that day with Mandunga Bula Niate, then the Minister of Communications and Information in the government of Zaire, and a firm friend of the Church. Also

Bay and Jean Hutchings
served mission in Zaire

present were Oscar W. McConkie of the Church's legal department and his wife, Judith, and a newly called missionary couple, R. Bay and Jean Hutchings. The group traveled to the home of President Mobutu Sese Seko, where their meeting and a subsequent interview with Elder Kennedy were recorded for television and radio. The interview was broadcast the next day to the people of Zaire.

At the time of their call to Zaire, Bay and Jean Hutchings certainly were no strangers to missionary work, Brother Hutchings having served previously as mission president in France and Switzerland. They promptly began to meet with Zairean investigators and the few members in the country — first in the carport of a member, Nkita Bungi Mbuyi, a returned missionary who had been converted in Belgium, and later in a large villa that was remodeled into a meetinghouse. The first baptisms in Zaire were the sons of Banza Muchioko and his wife, a

Zairean couple who had joined the Church in Switzerland several years previously.

By the time President and Sister Hutchings were released at the end of June 1988, a firm base had been laid for future growth in Zaire. Two large, well-organized branches were functioning in Kinshasa. Both were well housed—the Binza Branch in excellent rented quarters and the Limite Branch in an equally fine Church-owned building. Twelve hundred miles to the south, the Lubumbashi Branch, with over four hundred members, was approaching the point where division into two units could be considered.

On July 1, 1988, C. Stephen Hatch, a retired physician from Provo, Utah, became president of the Zaire Kinshasa Mission. President Hatch and his wife, Marjery, had previously served as missionaries in Mauritius and, before that, in Belgium, where he was the mission president. Wise, experienced, competent, and cool, he came to Zaire with a firm vision of where the mission was in terms of progress and where further development is required.

Many Latter-day Saints in Zaire are poor. Most families eat once a day if they are lucky and if someone in the family is working. Yet they exhibit the same spiritual strength and faithfulness so characteristic of other African Saints. Some time ago, for example, a Protestant minister named Baende Isukongola, with a strong congregation in Kinshasa, began to have serious misgivings about the teachings of his church. As he searched the scriptures, Baende noted numerous teachings and practices that were missing from the church he belonged to. Among other problems he became concerned that his church did not teach or practice tithing. He investigated the teachings and practices of other churches but found them also to be incomplete. Then a friend mentioned to Baende that a group he knew only as "the Mormons" evidently preached and practiced tithing. The minister finally established the fact that the Mormons had their world headquarters in the United States. He enlisted the assistance of the U.S. Embassy in Kinshasa, which directed him to the Zaire Kinshasa Mission.

One day Baende arrived on the doorstep of the mission home, anxious to learn about The Church of Jesus Christ of Latter-day Saints. Each week, armed with a long list of penetrating questions, he met with the missionaries. Soon the Spirit bore testimony to him and he was baptized. He brought his wife to hear the missionaries, and she too joined the Church, as did their two sons. One problem, however, had arisen. Knowing what he knew, Baende could not remain as a Protestant minister, and so he resigned his post. He had to give away a guaranteed income, a secure, assured source of livelihood, but he was glad to do so, realizing that he had found a pearl of great price, a splendrous treasure. It took great courage, in a country with unemployment rates of over 80 percent, to give up a job with no assurance at all that he would ever work again. Then a miracle happened. Baende obtained a permanent, secure job with the government. In the midst of all the unemployment in Zaire, he had again secured his temporal future. Two weeks later one of his sons also secured employment. The good brother recognized the hand of the Lord in his life and testified often of God's goodness to him. He and his family remain faithful members of the Church.

Sierra Leone

Missionary work in Sierra Leone began in 1988, when Elder C. Erwin Waite and his wife, Colleen, and Elder Clair Fisher and his wife, Iliene, arrived in that small, very poor West African country. The first few weeks were very difficult for the Waites and the Fishers as they struggled to find their way through the steamy disorder of Freetown, the capital of Sierra Leone. Their housing was inadequate. Though large enough, the house stood at the end of a dirt road, well nigh impassable after a rain. The electrical supply failed repeatedly, and there was no air conditioning. They also struggled with sickness and isolation. But through it all their courage remained high and their faith strong. They hung on and persevered. Things began to get better. More acceptable housing was found and electrical generators were purchased to ensure a reliable electricity source. Illness abated, perhaps in part because their housing conditions were improved.

The faith and courage of these missionaries is exemplified in the following excerpts from one of their recent monthly reports:

> We are busy teaching new contacts.
>
> We are preparing for another baptism on Saturday, September 10.
>
> We just can't teach fast enough.
>
> We want to develop leadership first, and will be applying soon for another branch here as soon as we can develop the necessary leadership.
>
> The work here is great, the people are the best, and we just love what we are doing.
>
> I hope we can do what the Lord wants us to do.

How blessed we are to have people like the Waites and the Fishers serving as missionaries for the Lord Jesus Christ! They typify a valiant band of missionary couples serving throughout Africa—facing challenges, to be sure, but secure in the knowledge they are on the Lord's errand and encircled about in the arms of His love. They are modern pioneers, the present-day equivalent of those who in the early days of the Church placed all that they had on the altar of service. Praise be to God that the spirit of service lives yet in the Church! The willingness of couple missionaries to serve and sacrifice in African countries such as Sierra Leone tells much not only about the devotion and commitment of the missionaries involved, but also about the power of the work—the power of a cause greater than mortal man, a cause that has a "more powerful effect upon the minds of the people than the sword, or anything else." (Alma 30:5; emphasis added.)

Kenya

The Church is not yet legally recognized in Kenya, so we have no missionaries there. Since 1981 Church representatives have looked after our interests in that East African country. Our current (1990) district president is Joseph Sitati, an extremely competent and spiritual Kenyan businessman. The Spirit broods over Kenya, however, as over other countries in Black Africa, preparing its people for the day when the fullness of the gospel will be preached with power and authority in that beautiful country. The following story illustrates the point.

In early 1988 Marvin Bowden, who was then serving as Church representative in Kenya, was summoned to a meeting with a district commissioner of the Kenyan government. This official, whose title is a holdover from British colonial days, is, in effect, the senior government representative in the district involved. As such he has the full weight of the government behind him. Since the Church is not yet recognized in Kenya, Brother Bowden was somewhat apprehensive about the meeting. His fears were heightened when the official said to him sharply, "You people are not even registered as a church in Kenya, yet I understand you had 150 people at your meetings last Sunday. I want an explanation!" Then, slamming a copy of the Book of Mormon on the table, he shouted, "And I want to know about that book!"

Brother Bowden took the commissioner at his word and proceeded to tell him about "that book." It was, he said, a book about Christ, another witness for Him. It contained the record of a fallen people and had been translated by a prophet of God. The official listened intently. Made bold by his silence, Brother Bowden proceeded to teach him the first missionary discussion, then the second, and finally the third. The Spirit was strong as that humble missionary bore powerful testimony of the truth of the great latter-day work and of the Savior of the world.

Finally, the commissioner rose from his chair. His tone

133

now was gentle, his voice quiet. "You and your people are free to meet whenever and wherever you wish," he said. "If I can help personally, please let me know." He picked up the Book of Mormon and gently caressed its cover. "My wife and I will join the Church after we've finished reading it," he said.

In recounting this story, Brother Bowden said, "Elder Morrison, I don't even remember driving home from the meeting. I think I just floated home on a cloud of joy."

Such is the power of the work in Africa.

Zimbabwe

For much of its history the part of southern Africa now known as Zimbabwe has been intimately influenced by events occurring in what is now the Republic of South Africa. Fleeing the chaos caused in southern Africa in the early years of the nineteenth century by the expansionist policies of the great Zulu military genius Shaka, Bantu-speaking peoples of the Ndebele (or Matabele) tribe migrated to what now is southwestern Zimbabwe. There they carved out a pastoralist kingdom, driving out the Shona tribe. Over the next half-century, British and Afrikaner traders, hunters, and prospectors moved into the region from the south.

In 1889, the British South Africa Company was formed by Cecil Rhodes to colonize and develop the region. By the turn of the century the Ndebele and Shona tribes had been pacified, and in 1923 Southern Rhodesia was annexed by the British crown. After fifteen years of guerilla warfare, the white minority in Rhodesia formally agreed to multiracial elections, and in 1980 the current state of Zimbabwe was formed, with Robert Mugabe, a Shona, as prime minister. Of the current population of over eight million, probably fewer than one hundred thousand are whites.

The opening up of missionary work in Zimbabwe must be seen as an extension of that which began in 1953, when three missionaries climbed Lion's Head Mountain overlooking Cape

Town and dedicated South Africa to the preaching of the restored gospel of Jesus Christ. Missionary work began in southern Rhodesia in late 1950, when visas were granted to permit missionaries of the Church to enter the British-ruled Confederation of Rhodesia and Nyasaland. Four missionaries were assigned to the city of Bulawayo, in Matabeleland, and four others to the capital of Salisbury (now Harare), where white settlers had defended themselves several decades previously against the warriors of the Mashona people.

Within a few months missionary work was firmly established, with the first convert, Hugh Hodgekiss, being baptized early in 1951. Currently there are chapels in Harare, Bulawayo, and Kwe Kwe.

The Zimbabwe Harare Mission was organized on July 1, 1987, with Joseph Hamstead as mission president. An Englishman, President Hamstead had served as a stake president and as president of the London Temple. He and his wife, Margaret, a charming and spritely woman, have been outstanding ambassadors for the Church in Zimbabwe, gaining the respect and trust of senior officials in the Zimbabwe government. Under President Hamstead's leadership, significant expansion of missionary work has begun among black Zimbabweans. Given the racial makeup of the country, one can expect that most of the future growth of the Church in Zimbabwe will occur among our black brothers and sisters. White missionaries in Zimbabwe enter the country as teachers in the school system and are permitted to carry out religious duties only in their spare time, after their daily labor as teachers is finished.

Betty Ann Regenass is a single parent whose first exposure to the Church occurred when she and her two young daughters went to a BYU Program Bureau production in Bulawayo. Missionaries called on her. At first she was wary, until two members of the Church who happened to be insurance salesmen visited her to determine whether she wanted to purchase additional insurance. After some discussion they indicated she couldn't

Joseph Hamstead, first president of Zimbabwe mission, and his wife, Margaret, pose with member of Church in Zimbabwe

really afford more insurance, but one of them said he had something better to offer. He told Betty Ann about the Church. She resolved to learn more, and she and her family subsequently were fellowshipped by the insurance salesman and his family, had the missionary discussions, and attended meetings and various Church functions. Says she: "At last our lives seemed to have meaning and purpose, and we had a testimony of the truth of the gospel and of The Church of Jesus Christ of Latter-day Saints."

Betty Ann and her oldest daughter were baptized on August 28, 1976, and her younger daughter joined as soon as she was old enough. The older daughter subsequently attended Brigham Young University. Despite all of the trauma and horror of the civil war in Zimbabwe, which directly affected Betty Ann's family, she remains true to the faith — a believing and practicing Latter-day Saint.

In 1983 Christopher Mandwe was a young African student at a Methodist boarding school in Zimbabwe. He had a great desire to seek out religious truth and attended various Christian churches, but concluded that although all had some truth, each had something vital missing from its doctrines and practices.

After investigating and abandoning an interest in at least five other religious organizations, Christopher met missionaries of The Church of Jesus Christ of Latter-day Saints. Says he: "My eyes and mind were opened, and I knew I had found what I was looking for. Those were some of the most glorious times of my life. I felt the love of God. I had found something that was more precious and above everything."

Christopher soon joined the Church. Shortly afterward he had an experience, typical among Africans, that strengthened his testimony. "About two months after my baptism," he recalled, "my deceased maternal grandmother appeared to me in a dream and told me that there was indeed a living God and that Jesus was the very Christ, the living Son of God. She also told me that the Book of Mormon was true and that I had done the right thing in joining the Church. I then had a strong desire to serve a mission." Christopher returned in early 1988 from serving as a missionary in the England Manchester Mission. He is an outstanding young man whose experience is indicative of the spiritual sensitivity of the African people.

Swaziland

In the early nineteenth century, southern Africa underwent a convulsion of fear and blood let loose by the Zulu tribe, led by a despotic military genius named Shaka. In Shaka's hands, organized terror became an instrument of state policy. His armies, armed with the terrible stabbing spear, the assegai, swept away the other black tribes in the present South African province of Natal. Tribe after tribe was subjugated, its ruling family killed and its young men incorporated into Shaka's armies. Thousands died or fled as the ruthless Zulu war machine rolled south, west, and north. Pockets of resistance managed to survive in the northern hills. One such group, the Dlamini clan, became the rulers of modern-day Swaziland, a mountain kingdom bordered on three sides by South Africa and on the east by Mozambique.

The land area of Swaziland is less than 7,000 square miles, making it one of the smallest countries in Africa. With its mountains, high meadows, and beautiful scenery, Swaziland is sometimes termed "the Switzerland of Africa." More than 90 percent of the approximately 750,000 inhabitants are black Africans.

The Church of Jesus Christ of Latter-day Saints is not yet a decade old in Swaziland, Church meetings having been held in the country only since 1984. A branch was organized in 1986 with Brother John Scott, an expatriate resident of the country, as president. In 1987 the government officially reognized the Church as a legal entity. That same year the first Swazi members were baptized. By early 1990 there were approximately 120 members, all of whom are black Africans except the branch president, Larry Brown, and his family. Brother Brown is an American public health official on temporary assignment in Swaziland, seconded from the U.S. Centers for Disease Control. He and his family are among the great "nursing fathers and mothers" who are the Lord's pioneers in Africa, helping to establish the Church in one country after another.

In February 1990, Elder Neal A. Maxwell of the Council of the Twelve dedicated Swaziland for the preaching of the gospel and the work of the Lord. I was privileged to accompany Elder Maxwell on that historic occasion. The dedication ceremony, attended by local members and Church leaders from the South Africa Johannesburg Mission and the Benoni South Africa Stake, was held on a beautiful grassy hilltop overlooking the capital city of Mbabane. During the program a misty cloud settled over the hill like a soft wool blanket, effectively separating the small group on the Lord's errand from the bustling, noisy city below. It was as though He had drawn a curtain to shield sacred proceedings from worldly influences.

As reported in the *Church News* (March 10, 1990), Elder

Elder Alexander B. Morrison, left and Elder Neal A. Maxwell, right, with Church members at dedication of Swaziland in spring 1990

Maxwell, in an eloquent, deeply spiritual dedicatory prayer, blessed the country and its rulers and asked the Lord to bless the people with a testimony that the Book of Mormon is another testament of Jesus Christ. A sweet, gentle spirit touched the hearts of all present, and many rejoiced with the realization that in the rapturous rhythm of the Restoration, the time had come "for the fulness of the gospel to come to this good land and to this good people."

Lesotho

Lesotho, the "kingdom in the sky," lies in mountainous country in southern Africa, completely surrounded by the Republic of South Africa. It owes its existence to a chief named Mosheoshoe (Moe-shway-shway), a contemporary of Shaka, and the son of a minor chief of the Sotho tribe. In his early manhood Moshoeshoe experienced the terrible chaos caused by Zulu expansionism. Bands of Zulu marauders raided repeatedly through the mountains and valleys of what today is the country of Lesotho, leaving in their wake a swath of death and destruction. In the dead of winter, Moshoeshoe led his family and two hundred followers to refuge atop a mountain with a perennial spring at its summit. He was to remain in his mountain fortress for half a century, constantly growing in strength through a rare combination of diplomacy and force, playing his enemies off against one another with great skill and subtlety. Moshoeshoe was a remarkable man by any measure, revered to this day by his people as a leader of unusual strength and wisdom.

The Church of Jesus Christ of Latter-day Saints is in its infancy in Lesotho, having been recognized by the government in July 1989. The first baptisms took place in December 1989, and several foundation families have already joined the Church.

Elder Neal A. Maxwell of the Council of the Twelve dedicated Lesotho on February 22, 1990. Once again I was honored to accompany Elder Maxwell on the Lord's sacred errand.

The dedication took place late on a sunny afternoon in a pleasant grove of trees secluded from the world, near the capital city of Maseru. It was a place of gentle beauty. The afternoon sun, filtering through the leaves, bathed the grove in shimmering shadows, and in the background the Caledon River murmured and gurgled. I thought of another day and another sacred grove, far away from southern Africa, where the Father and Son appeared to a boy prophet and ushered in the last dispensation of the glorious gospel.

An eleven-year-old African boy, Tsuenvane Kutlane, solemnly and with great reverence read a brief history of his land and people. Overcome with emotion, he paused several times to wipe the tears from his eyes with the end of his necktie. I glanced at Elder Maxwell, he of the tender loving heart, and noted his eyes too were wet with emotion. So were my own.

In his eloquent dedicatory prayer, Elder Maxwell petitioned the God of heaven to "smile upon this smiling people,

African boy gives history of area while other boys watch at dedication of Lesotho, spring 1990

that their basic goodness, friendliness and happiness" would bring many of them to Christ. (*Church News,* March 10, 1990.) He prayed that Lesotho might be a "host country for a host of those who come here." His listeners were silent, struck by the solemnity of the occasion, and sensing that they were in the presence of a prophet, seer, and revelator.

The presiding elder in Lesotho at the time of its dedication was another expatriate pioneer in Africa, Gary Massey, who comes from Fresno, California. Brother Massey, an agronomist, is in Lesotho to direct a crop improvement project sponsored by the U.S. Agency for International Development. I was excited to see experimental plots where he is growing improved varieties of beans and other crops that will significantly increase the food supply in Lesotho. I thrilled to learn that the farmers of the region are anxious to adopt improved procedures and crop varieties. But even more thrilling was to see Brother and Sister Massey's loving, gentle warmth toward their African brothers and sisters. It was a lesson on the gospel in action.

CHAPTER NINE

The Dawning of a New Day in Africa

I have proclaimed boldly in this book that with the coming of The Church of Jesus Christ of Latter-day Saints to Africa, a new day has dawned on that great continent. But is it all presumptuous claptrap or sentimental nonsense? Can Africa ever truly be free from her ancient enemies? Can the myriad peoples of that vast land, hounded and harried for so long by the grim quartet of poverty, ignorance, disease, and famine, ever escape from their implacable pursuers? Or is the dream of a better day, a brighter future in sunny uplands of peace and joy, but an illusion, a chimera, a pipe dream turned nightmare by the dashing of hopes, the death of aspirations? Is it realistic to speak of a better day in the face of the grinding poverty and stultifying ignorance that still grip Africa; the corruption and venality that siphon away precious resources needed for development and besmirch all who are touched by them; the crushing economic burdens and lack of technical competence that shackle African governments; the grisly spectre of AIDS hovering obscenely behind the ancient scourges that continue to foreclose the future for millions? Even the most optimistic observers have their doubts.

Yet with it all, in spite of it all, a new and better day *is* dawning over Africa. That is my simple faith. It is a day whose light is the Son of God, a day made brighter by the glow of the glorious gospel of Christ. It is a day when the power of the priesthood of God, the power by which the universe itself was formed and put into place, is being exercised to lift, leaven, and exalt people long shackled and held powerless. The light of the restored gospel falls on a prepared people—a people prepared by the Spirit of God to receive the Word. It dispels the spiritual gloom and drives away the shadows of error and superstition that long have lain like a black shroud over the "dark continent."

The words of Alma, uttered in a different context, come to mind: "The Lord did pour out his Spirit on all the face of the land to prepare the minds of the children of men, or to prepare their hearts to receive the word which should be taught among them . . . that they might not be hardened against the word, that they might not be unbelieving, and go on to destruction, but that they might receive the word with joy, and as a branch be grafted into the true vine, that they might enter into the rest of the Lord their God." (Alma 16:16–17.)

Let us have no illusions: the task will not be easy. The road will be long and arduous. Many are the obstacles to be torn down, the challenges to be won. God's authorized servants will require all of the skills and talents they can muster to achieve success, and will be driven repeatedly to their knees in humble supplication for the aid of the powers of heaven to give them the endowment of wisdom required.

The work cannot be done overnight. The peoples of Africa must be taught the riches of the gospel of Christ by those authorized to do so. They will need help—nursing fathers and nursing mothers who can bring Africa's sons in their arms and carry her daughters upon their shoulders for a season. (See 1 Nephi 21:22.) That help, the training and teaching required, must be done in the spirit of loving kindliness and fraternal cooperation, as one would help a brother or sister in need, and not out of any misguided and ignorant assumption of superiority. There must be no patronizing, no treatment of

143

Africans as children, no spoon-feeding. The task will be completed only when Africa can stand on her own feet, when her people can take their rightful place in God's kingdom, bold, noble, and independent.

Why the optimism in the face of grim reality? The answer will no doubt seem simpleminded to many. The truth often does. A new day is dawning over Africa because God in His wisdom wills it to be so, and that makes all the difference. In many ways the key to it all — or at least the signal of divine intentions — was the revelation on the priesthood in 1978. That symbol of God's love for all of His children signified that a critical point had been reached in the divine timetable for earth and its inhabitants, and that the time had come to call up the last laborers to serve in the vineyard of the Lord.

The first glorious rays of sunlight (or perhaps more appropriately Son-light) are penetrating the night of ages past. The clouds of a long night's darkness are beginning to roll away from Africa as a new day dawns. The work of bringing souls to Christ in Africa will roll on, slowly at first, but steadily gathering strength and power "till the purposes of God shall be accomplished, and the Great Jehovah shall say, the work is done." (Joseph Smith, "The Wentworth Letter," in *History of the Church* 4:540.)

Bibliography

Those who are interested in additional general information about historical and contemporary Africa may wish to read the following selected texts. (If I could read only one book, it would be that of David Lamb.)

Davidson, Basil. *The Story of Africa.* London: Mitchell Beazley Publishers, 1984.

De Villiers, Marq. *White Tribe Dreaming.* London: Penguin Books, 1987.

Fage, J. D. *A History of Africa.* 2d ed. London: Hutchinson, 1988.

Hanley, Gerald. *Warriors and Strangers.* London: Hamish Hamilton, 1987.

Hibbert, Christopher. *Africa Explored: Europeans in the Dark Continent, 1769–1889,* London: Penguin Books, 1984.

Lamb, David. *The Africans.* New York: Vintage Books, 1987.

Magrui, Ali A. *The Africans, a Triple Heritage.* Boston: Little, Brown & Company, 1986.

Parrinder, E. J. *African Traditional Religion.* 3d ed. London: Sheldon Press, 1974.

Ransford, Oliver. *"Bid the Sickness Cease": Disease in the History of Black Africa.* London: John Murray, 1983.

Unger, Sanford J. *Africa, The People and Politics of an Emerging Continent.* New York: Simon & Schuster, Inc., 1986.

Index